ACCLAIM FOR LAURA FRASER'S

AN ITALIAN AFFAIR

"[Fraser's] sexy memoir gives new meaning to the word *wanderlust*."
—*Glamour*

"Part travel writing, part erotica, *An Italian Affair* will transport you to the Amalfi Coast faster than a glass of pinot gris."
—*The Boston Phoenix*

"Dreamy, romantic, spiced with the exotic, just a little bit indulgent. . . . It's an intoxicating trip."
—*The Star-Ledger*

"A sharp-eyed romantic, [Fraser] gives her story a freshness and intimacy that makes her book impossible to put down."
—*Palo Alto Daily News*

"Dotted with sumptuous details about food, scenery, and the landscape of the human heart."
—*Woman's Own*

"In a perfect world, all romance novels would read like *An Italian Affair*. . . . Fraser is an unusually generous memoirist. When she gets lucky so do her readers."
—*Salon*

"A charming travelogue . . . [Fraser] writes beautifully, one might even say lustily."
—*Chicago Sun-Times*

LAURA FRASER

AN ITALIAN AFFAIR

Laura Fraser has written for Salon.com, *Vogue*, *Glamour*, *Mother Jones*, *Self*, *San Francisco Examiner*, *Gourmet*, and *Health*, among other publications. She has taught magazine writing at the Graduate School of Journalism at the University of California at Berkeley. She lives in San Francisco.

ALSO BY LAURA FRASER

Losing It: False Hopes and Fat Profits in the Diet Industry

AN
ITALIAN
AFFAIR

LAURA FRASER

VINTAGE BOOKS

A Division of Random House, Inc.

New York

FIRST VINTAGE BOOKS EDITION, MAY 2002

Portions of this work were previously published in essay format on the Internet
media site Salon.com (12/2/97 and 9/29/98) and subsequently in the book
Salon.com's Wanderlust: Real-Life Tales of Adventure and Romance edited
by Don George (Villard Books, New York, 2000).

The Library of Congress has cataloged the Pantheon edition as follows:
Fraser, Laura.
An Italian affair / Laura Fraser.
p. cm.
ISBN 0-375-42065-7
1. Fraser, Laura. 2. Divorced women—United States—Biography. 3. Man-woman
relationships—Case studies. 4. Fraser, Laura—Journeys—Italy.
5. Italy—Description and travel. I. Title.
HQ834.F73 2001
306.7'092—dc21
00-052881

Vintage ISBN: 0-375-72485-0

Author photograph © Christina Taccone
Book design by Johanna S. Roebas

www.vintagebooks.com

Printed in the United States of America
10 9 8 7 6 5 4 3

To M.

And it pleased Him that this love of mine,
whose warmth exceeded all others, and which had stood firm
and unyielding against all the pressures of good intention,
helpful advice, and the risk of danger and open scandal,
should in the course of time diminish of its own accord.
So that now, all that is left of it in my mind is the delectable
feeling which Love habitually reserves for those who
refrain from venturing too far upon its deepest waters.
And thus what was once a source of pain has now become,
having shed all discomfort, an abiding sensation of pleasure.

—GIOVANNI BOCCACCIO,
THE DECAMERON

AN ITALIAN AFFAIR

SAN FRANCISCO

Mi hai spaccato il cuore.

You're reading a fairy tale in your evening Italian class when you come across this phrase. You think you know what it means, since the sea princess says it after her one true love abandons her, but you ask the teacher anyway.

"You have broken my heart," he says, and he makes a slashing motion diagonally across his dark blue sweater. "You have cloven it in two."

Mi hai spaccato il cuore.

The phrase plays over and over in your mind, and the words in front of you blur. You can see your husband's face with his dark, wild eyebrows, and you whisper the phrase to him, *Mi hai spaccato il cuore.* You say it to plead with him, to make him stay, and then you say it with heat, a wronged Sicilian fishwife with a dagger in her hand. But he doesn't understand, he doesn't speak Italian; you shared so many things in your marriage, but Italy was all yours.

Mi hai spaccato il cuore.

You hear the phrase so many times that it loses its meaning, it just becomes Italian music, and it takes you into another realm. You're in another world, a place where people linger over lunch, drink full-bodied coffee, and stroll arm-in-arm at sunset. A place where the towns are built on such thick layers of tragedy and romance, stacked up like stones, that you can't take anything that happens to you very seriously. A place where you wouldn't be worried about running into your husband, who left you after a year of marriage for an old girlfriend, at an intimate little restaurant in your neighborhood. Where you wouldn't be home making dinner, expecting to hear the thumping sound of him doing fast-paced yoga in the bedroom upstairs. Where you wouldn't walk into the bathroom in the morning and miss having to pick up the Scotch glass and wet mystery novel he left behind on the ledge of the tub the night before. In Italy, you would be far away.

Mi hai spaccato il cuore.

Let's say you have a few friends in Italy and you speak the language well enough. Maybe you could go there, just drift away from all of this and leave it behind. Maybe you would feel more like yourself again. Why not? And then a fantasy flickers and you think perhaps an Italian man might not be such a bad idea, either.

Someone speaks to you and you look up and see bright blue eyes with smile lines and a head of gray-black curls. Your Italian teacher. He puts a hand on your shoulder and you realize you are crying.

"Laura," your teacher asks. *"Che c'è?"* What's up?

You quickly wipe your eyes and gather up your books. *"Mi dispiace tanto, ma devo andarmene,"* you say. I'm so sorry, but I have to leave.

{ONE}

FLORENCE

When the plane touches down in Florence, it's evening. Lucia is there, waving from outside the security area, flipping her short dark hair away from her angular face. She kisses you on both cheeks and says you look great, even though that can't possibly be true. She speaks Italian faster than you can understand in your bleary condition, but you're glad to just follow along. Lucia loads your bag into her miniature car and goes careening around the perimeter of the city and into the center.

Just outside the pedestrian zone, she maneuvers into a tiny parking spot, and you walk from there along the narrow cobblestone streets until you reach a *pensione* right in the historic center, near the Piazza della Signoria. You're staying at a little hotel this visit because Lucia, an art teacher who was divorced, unhappily, in her late thirties, has a new boyfriend who stays over. So there's no more room at her place. You don't mind; Lucia seems so content, her face softer than the last time you saw her.

You ring at a massive wooden door, get buzzed in, and then squeeze into an elevator cage that barely fits the two of you and your bag. You greet the grumpy signora at the front desk, roused from her TV napping, and deposit your things. It's late, but Lucia insists you have to go out for a drink.

"Andiamo," she says, and you are glad to be persuaded.

You return to the streets, which, despite the hour, are filled with couples strolling, middle-aged signoras locking arms, tourists taking flash photos, and bands of teenagers gathered on the steps of the magnificent marble Duomo. You end up at one of the cafés on the Piazza della Repubblica, taking a seat at an outdoor table, the September night air still warm. The waiter comes up in his crisp white shirt and black bow tie, and without asking, Lucia orders you both glasses of spumante secco.

The spumante secco reminds you of a moment you shared the year before, when you were vacationing together for a few days in the Cinque Terre, on the Ligurian coast, hiking from one fishing village to the next. You had arrived in Manarola, with its pastel houses stacked up around a tiny harbor, and sat down, dusty and tired, for a drink before dinner. Lucia had ordered the spumante, and by the time the waiter set the glasses down the sun was just setting beyond the little harbor, turning the whole sea as pink as smooth sandstone. *"La vita è un' arte,"* she'd said, clinking glasses.

You had returned to that moment in your mind many times since, to cheer you up.

When the waiter brings the drinks, Lucia clicks glasses with you again. *"Cin cin,"* she says, chin chin. Then she gets right down to business, asking what happened with your husband.

"Raccontami tutto," she says. The Italians have that wonderful verb, *raccontare,* that means to tell a story. Tell me the story about everything.

She says she can't imagine how it happened. Just the year

before, she reminds you, when you'd stayed with her for a few weeks, your new husband was always calling from San Francisco, just to tell you he loved you. In return, you had sent him cards you made with photo booth pictures, wearing Italian movie star sunglasses, blowing kisses, *ciao ciao,* telling him he was the only reason you didn't stay in Florence forever.

"What happened?" Lucia asks.

You say you aren't really sure, you're still in a state of shock about the whole thing. You recount, as best you can in your night-school Italian, the bare details of the breakup. You'd been married just over a year, after being together for three years before that. He had a new job as a trial attorney, and you'd just had your first book out; you were both doing what you'd always wanted to do with your lives. Everything seemed to be fine, even if you were both very busy. Then suddenly, just as mysteriously as you had fallen in love four years before, he seemed to fall out of love.

"When did it start, this falling out of love?" asks Lucia, sipping her drink.

You don't know. You had been luxuriating in your new marriage and didn't see the signs of trouble. Maybe it was in February, on your birthday, when you first became aware of a rift between you. You had driven north of San Francisco to Point Reyes National Seashore. That was the place, you tell Lucia, that had reminded her of the Sardinian coast when she visited you there. It was the place your husband and you had hiked when you were first so amazed that you'd found each other. On that day in February, on the trail back from the estuary where you had watched some sea lions lounge in the winter sun with their pups, you brought up the topic of having a child. Your husband—let's call him Jon—said he wasn't sure it was a good

7

time. You said it's probably never a good time, but you had talked about it for a couple of years, and at thirty-six, you can't wait forever. He was quiet for a while before telling you that if you did get pregnant, it would really freak him out.

"But he wanted to have children?" Lucia asks.

"Yeah, that's why we decided to get married."

Lucia blows out smoke with a sigh.

"I was so sure we were going to have a child," you tell her, "that I even bought a set of maternity clothes." You had never confessed that to anyone before. They were still in the back of your closet, because you couldn't stand to give them away.

"You already bought maternity clothes?" asked Lucia. "*Sei pazza, cara.*" You're crazy, my dear. She takes a long look at you and shakes her head. "Well," she says, waving her cigarette, "you can always wear them if you get really fat."

"*Perfetto!*" you say, laughing for the first time in months. "Do they serve *gelato* here?" you joke, scanning the restaurant for the waiter. Then your eyes rest back on Lucia, who has stopped smiling. "I was stupid," you say.

"You weren't stupid. You wanted a *bambino.* That's natural. Go on."

That day on the hike, the conversation shifted subtly, crucially. Jon said he wasn't just freaked out about having a baby in general. He was freaked out about you having a baby together. In that one moment, the whole relationship was in question, everything was up for grabs, and he couldn't explain why.

In the weeks after that, Jon got up earlier every morning to go to work, and stayed later after work at the gym. It also turned out that he was seeing a lot of a high school girlfriend, who, after being out of touch for twenty years, had called out of the blue. That explained why Jon, who had been too tired for months to make love at nine-thirty, was now coming home sometimes at one in the morning.

"He was seeing another woman?" asks Lucia, her bright face darkening. "Did you know her?"

You had met her once. You came home from being out with a friend one evening to find the remains of a cozy dinner, with candles and flowers. You called, and no one answered. You went upstairs to the bedroom, dreading the worst, and found them out on the terrace outside. They were wrapped in sleeping bags, drinking wine, staring at the moon.

"He *knew* you were coming home and he was there with another woman? In camping bags?" asked Lucia, incredulous. "What did you do?"

"I introduced myself." She left quickly, and the rest was a blur of discussions and lies, even a broken plate (you threw it, of course). Suddenly you were in the third session with a marriage counselor where your husband said, flatly, I just want out of this relationship. He didn't even call it a marriage. He dropped you off at home with an anxious, gripping hug, both of you crying, and that was it. He left.

"That was four months ago," you tell Lucia, "in May."

"I'm so sorry," says Lucia.

You're quiet for a moment, and then she makes a gesture flicking her fingers under her chin that Italians use to say, economically, forget him, he wasn't worth it, life goes on and you'll be better off.

"He seemed like he was an interesting, intelligent man," Lucia says, "but he never had the love of life you have anyway, the sense of *la bella vita*."

You nod. Lucia is right. There's nothing more to say. You drain your glass, and Lucia gestures for another round.

"You'll find someone else, someone better," Lucia says. "I never thought I would at first, but eventually, I did. It may not have been in time for a family, but . . ." She sips her spumante. *"Però, è così."*

You lift your glass to Lucia. "To your new love," you say. She smiles.

"And to yours. When he comes."

The next morning, you wander around your favorite places in Florence. You stroll in the Boboli Gardens, hiking to the top, where the view of the city's spires, domes, and red-tiled roofs has always awed you. But now it just looks like another postcard.

You walk back down through the park, taking winding paths that lead to the streets, and study the windows of the boutiques near the Ponte Vecchio. You pass the men's store where the year before a charming salesman had spent half an hour helping you choose among the most beautiful ties in Italy, holding each one up under his chin, while you tried to decide which one you should send home to your husband. The tie you eventually agreed on had looked great on the Italian, and your husband had liked it, too—as much, anyway, as he ever liked a piece of clothing. When you met him, he had little regard for his appearance: aviator glasses, Grateful Dead T-shirts, bushy black hair, floodwater jeans. Beautiful smile, though. After living with you, he'd cut his hair, bought new glasses, some clothes that fit, and he'd received a lot of gorgeous ties. So now he looks great for his new girlfriend. And you look, well, older.

Next door, a boutique is just opening after lunch. You don't ordinarily go into Italian boutiques, not only because their clothes are usually made for tiny people, but because if you go inside it shows you're serious about buying something. You can't just browse the way you can in the United States. You nod hello to the shopkeeper, a stylish woman in her forties with a long black mane, and glance at the colorful shirts stacked in twos and threes on minimalist glass shelves. When you were together, your husband had definite ideas about what he liked you to wear: nothing too colorful or sexy, lots of navy blue, anything with a polo collar, sensible shoes. For a free-spirited type, he had extremely Princetonian taste in women's clothing. It was as if he'd been attracted to you for your exuberance, and then did everything he could to tone it down. You dutifully chucked your red shoes into the back of the closet and wore a lot of gray.

You ask the shopkeeper if you can try on a short magenta jacket. She looks at you doubtfully. "I don't think it will work on you," she concludes. Unlike in the United States, where clerks will sell you anything, no matter how unflattering, Italian shopkeepers don't want to be responsible for any aesthetic errors walking around on the streets.

"Why not?" you ask her.

"Signora," she says, delicately, "you have a large bottom and a small waist, and a short jacket will not look good on you. You must always wear a long jacket, fitted in here," she says, gesturing to your waist.

She was right, of course. What were you thinking? You should never deviate from that slenderizing long-jacket rule. You also never should have walked in. They have nothing your size in that store, nothing big enough for you and your big bottom.

The shopkeeper, sensing that you are out of sorts, whirls around to another rack, sifts through, and hands you a bronze knit top with tiny skin-baring stripes of crochet woven in. "This will suit you," she says. You try it on, half-heartedly, but it's a little too clingy, a little bare. You emerge from the dressing room and stand, slumped, in front of her. "It doesn't work on me."

She studies you. "The color is good for your hair, it picks up the gold, and the brown in your eyes."

"It's a little too sexy," you say doubtfully.

The shopkeeper gives you a look that suggests that nothing can ever be too sexy. "Well, you can wear a little camisole underneath it if you must," she says, pulling at the fabric here and there. "And you have to stand up, hold yourself strong." You straighten up a bit. "There," she says, "you have a beautiful bust, you should show it off."

You turn in front of the mirror. "This makes me look fat."

The *commessa* throws up her hands. "You are a woman, you have a woman's body, so what?" she says. "You should show what's nice about your body. I think your husband will like this."

He certainly wouldn't have liked it. "I don't have a husband," you tell her, fingering the fabric.

"Well, then, it's good to dress sexy for yourself," she says. "Maybe even better."

"D'accordo." Yes. You could dress sexy for yourself. You walk out with a top that your husband definitely would have hated, for about the price of a really nice tie.

The next day, you wake up questioning why you're in Italy. It's September, your friends are all busy working, and you have no plans. You've been to Florence before, you've seen all the major museums and monuments already, but you distract yourself by being a tourist anyway. You wait with all the other tourists, a long line of ants, to finally get into the Uffizi, crowding around the

Botticellis and Titians, trying to catch a glimpse of the paintings between all the elbows and shoulders.

You really aren't in the mood for any more museums, so you rent a bicycle and ride up to Fiesole, past villas and vineyards, past the cliff where Leonardo da Vinci made some hapless assistant test out his first flying machine, and all the way to the top of the hill. The view everywhere is stupendous—cypress trees and olive terraces, Florence at your feet—but you can't just sit there and admire it. You're impatient to move on, to coast back down to town as fast as you can. No matter where you go, you always have the sense that something is following you close behind.

The following morning, you don't care that you're in Italy, you can't get out of bed. You're as tearful and depressed as you'd been in San Francisco; you've come all this way and all you can think about is how much you miss your husband, and how there's no one to call if you want to call home. At lunchtime, it's all you can do to finally get up and go see your friend Nina at her office near Santa Croce.

Nina is on the phone when you arrive, arguing with someone, gesturing angrily with one hand and greeting you effusively with the other. She drops the phone and runs over to embrace you, kissing you quickly on both cheeks, giving her assistant some instructions over your shoulder. Nina picks up her perfect black jacket and trim leather bag and motions you to come on, follow her out.

Nina, a sophisticated woman in her forties, stayed with you in San Francisco for a month several years ago, a friend of your Italo-American friend Cecilia, who had lived in Italy years before. At the time, you spoke no Italian, but Nina spoke a little English, and you communicated well enough that you admired her sensibility. She would make big bowls of exquisitely savory pasta, even though she swore she couldn't cook. She felt so sorry for your boyfriend then, for going out with a vegetarian, that she once made him a steak *and* a roast for dinner. She ate lunch every day at the same Italian restaurant in the neighborhood, and said she had absolutely no desire to go anywhere else, to venture out to try Thai, Cambodian, or Vietnamese food because there was always a risk of getting cilantro in a dish, and cilantro tastes like soap. A petite, dark-haired woman with a smoky voice, Nina had brought few clothes with her, but always dressed impeccably in a wool skirt, twin set, and flat Italian loafers—even just to go to her English language classes. She couldn't understand the way her American friend dressed, and once opened up your closet and demanded to know why you went around in sloppy jeans all the time when you had a wardrobe full of beautiful clothes. *"Non ha senso,"* she said. It makes no sense.

A year later, Nina's friend—and now your friend—Lucia came to visit San Francisco with a group of her girlfriends. You had big dinner parties at your flat, everyone's cheeks red with wine and laughter. They invited you to stay with them in a house in Monterey that they'd managed to exchange for a week for one of their places in Italy. You went hiking with Lucia in Big Sur—she was the only one of the Italian women who was interested in hiking—and you liked that she was so willing to be awed by the drama of the steep coastal mountains, and by the playful sea lions at the rocky beach. Even though you spoke only Spanish in common, you became great friends, closer than most friends you'd known in San Francisco for years. There was something *simpatico* between you.

After the Italian women went home, you decided to try to learn the language, taking one evening class after another and watching all the Marcello Mastroianni films you could get your hands on. You took advantage of having friends and a free place to stay and visited Nina and Lucia in Florence a couple of times over the years. You became familiar with Florence, knowing the bus routes and flea markets and out-of-the-way restaurants where only Italians ate. You went to cooking school for a week in a fourteenth-century villa in Tuscany, spending mornings making ravioli and risotto, and afternoons walking on dusty paths through vineyards, olive groves, and patches of purple thistles. Then it was two weeks in a language school overlooking the Arno in Florence, drilling *passato remoto* verbs with young Swiss students who were much more serious than you were, but who managed to make the language sound guttural and stiff. You went to a Bob Dylan concert in a medieval town square outside of Florence, your Italian friends insisting that you translate the lyrics, and then laughing when you tried, "all confused in a big mess of blue."

By the time Lucia's friend Giovanna came to San Francisco to stay for a month—nothing an Italian would ever consider an imposition, and so you didn't, either—you'd learned enough of the language to carry on a decent conversation and slowly, slowly improved.

Now Nina leads you from her office into a busy little stand-up lunch place, where everyone crowds around the bar trying to shout his or her order. The guy behind the bar ignores everyone else when Nina approaches the counter. He asks what La Nina would like today, and she asks him what's good. They have a long, flirtatious conversation while everyone else tries to catch the waiter's attention. Finally Nina orders and steers you to a wobbly high table by the window, setting down a couple of glasses of red wine and then going back to the bar to pick up the plates of pasta. Nina tries a bite of the simple *penne* with fresh tomatoes and basil and exclaims about how good it is, thrilled at her choice, even though she eats at that same place every single day.

Nina says she was sorry to hear about your separation. "The first time you're heartbroken is always the worst," she assures you, dismissing the topic, and then asks about your vacation so far. You tell her about the exhibits and museums you've seen, and she is as excited talking about the art that surrounds her every day as she is about her lunch.

She shakes her head, marveling. "Laura, Laura," she says. "Last time you were here, you said you would learn Italian, and now you've learned it!"

"I need practice," you say.

"You need an Italian lover," Nina replies, matter-of-factly. "That's the only solution." Nina lights a cigarette, considering that. "To everything."

You tell her it's not such a bad idea. More than anything, you say, just realizing it, you want to put a body between yourself and your husband. You don't want him to be the last person you made love to, especially since the last time had been so horrible.

Nina asked why it had been so bad, and you tell her, because it's somehow easy to tell intimate stories in a romance language. It was during the brief period when your husband and you had been tense with each other; he was on his way out of the relationship, and you were trying to hang on, still thinking it was just a difficult time, the kind of thing couples go through that ends up making their marriages stronger. You thought maybe if you made love, things would be better, you would reconnect. You had joked about it, saying it could just be like casual sex, and he reluctantly agreed. After you'd had sex, mechanical sex, you leaned over his face to kiss him, and he turned away. "No," he'd said. "You're not supposed to kiss on the lips."

Nina gasps. *"Incredibile."*

Afterward, you got up to take a shower, pounding hot, to wash the whole thing away, and you knew that it was the last time you'd ever make love to your husband.

"That's terrible when you know it's the last time," Nina says. "But you always know." Nina drags on her cigarette and blows the smoke out the side of her mouth. "After that experience, the angels made a special note that you deserve better next time. I'm sure."

"Speriamo di sì," you say. Let's hope so. You pick at your pasta and tell Nina you're glad Lucia seems happy with her new boyfriend, since Lucia had been depressed after she split up with her husband—although it's hard to read depression in someone who is always so energetic and quick to laugh. You ask Nina if she is seeing anyone herself, and Nina waves away the question, too silly to consider. Then she confesses that she's been dating a musician, and starts laughing at herself.

"He's fat!" Nina bursts out. "I've never been with a fat man before!" She leans closer and whispers. "It's like riding waves," she says. "Wonderful!"

You like that image, and the way your Italian friends appreciate sensuality in all types, forget the ideal. You tell Nina that you yourself are cursed with always having skinny men interested in you. "Opposites attract," you say.

Nina looks at your body in that frank way Italian women will size you up. "You're thinner than you were last year," she observes.

It's the divorce, you explain. For the first time in your life, you've had no interest in food.

"Eat your pasta," Nina commands, and you do, glad that your appetite is returning.

As you wait for the waiter to bring coffee, Nina asks what you intend to do for the rest of your vacation. You tell her you don't know; you realize it's a bad time to be in Italy, your friends are all busy, and you've spent enough time in Florence over the years that you don't need another week dodging tour groups and looking at church interiors. You leave out that it's too hard to be in a place where your friends are all in love. You want to visit Giovanna in Bologna, but she, too, was recently married, and so you really can't stay there long, either. You don't have a plan for cooking school or a language course. You've already been to Rome, Venice, Ravenna, Umbria, Bologna, Liguria, and Tuscany. Maybe you'll go somewhere new.

Nina slaps her elegant little hand on the table. *"Napoli!"* she says, pleased with herself. "Perfect!" She'd just been to Naples, and had a wonderful time. The old architecture, the sense of beauty amidst decay, the food—it was all wonderful.

You're surprised. You'd always heard that Naples was a dangerous city to travel in, especially for a woman alone.

Nina waves away that concern. "It's like New York," she says. "If you carry your camera in a plastic bag, keep your money close to you, and act like you know what you're doing, you'll be fine."

"Maybe," you say.

"And Ischia!" Nina exclaims, ignoring your reluctance. "Go to Naples, look around the old city—you must look around—and then get the ferry to Ischia." Nina is definite, and full of plans, describing the island. "Or you can take the ferry from

Pozzuoli, if you like. You can also go to Amalfi, to Pompeii . . ." Nina ticks off the possibilities on her fingers. "Just don't go to Capri. Capri is crawling with tourists, and way too expensive. You'll pay ten thousand lire there just for a cappuccino." Nina downs her espresso in one gulp. She has solved all of your problems, so she checks her watch. She has to get back to work.

You walk back to Nina's office, half a block away, and kiss good-bye. Nina runs up the stone steps to the grand front door of her building, then turns around. "Ischia, Laura," she calls, waving. "Ischia."

And so, the next day, you set out for Ischia. Maybe you'll see Naples, Capri, Pompeii, and the Amalfi coast, too, but your sights are set on Ischia. Something about a volcanic island with natural hot baths and long pebbly beaches sounds about right. Everything will be white stucco and washed with Mediterranean light. Everything else will be far, far away.

{TWO}

ISCHIA

In the morning, you catch an express train for Naples. You're lulled by the motion of the train, passing dreamy sunlit fields with villages teetering atop the distant hills.

An Italian high school student sits across from you in your compartment, reading Jack London. You greet him and ask him how he likes the book, telling him that Jack London used to live near where you live in California. He shyly asks you about the American West, whether it's still wild, full of gun-slinging bandits and grizzly bears. Gun-slinging bandits, yes, you tell him; grizzly bears, not so many. You tell him stories about 14,000-foot mountains, ghost towns, rattlesnakes, sport utility vehicles, and urban sprawl with endless shopping malls, and then ask him what he knows about Naples. He says he's never been there; he's heard it's beautiful but full of thieves. It isn't a place, he advises, for a woman to travel alone. He says good-bye and gets out in Rome.

The further south of Rome the train travels, the more it looks like another, older, more battered world. The buildings all seem either half built or half falling down, and you can't tell which is which. You've heard that Naples isn't so much the southernmost city in mainland Europe as the northernmost city in Africa—even if Marcello Mastroianni once said that the people there are the most civilized in the world.

When the train finally pulls into Napoli, the station seems crowded and seedy. Outside, the traffic is zipping around without rules. The grimy buildings have all seen better days. Part of you wants to charge out of the station to explore Napoli, to take in its light and liveliness, to meet some of those people who are renowned for having suffered through so much adversity that they can laugh at anything. But you're also nervous. You figure you'll be safe; you've brought only a day pack with a few things—a swimsuit, a sweater, a toothbrush, a change of clothes, a disposable camera, a few pages from a guidebook—so there's nothing to steal. You'll make your way around just fine. But you have no map and no place to stay, and while those will be easy enough to find, somehow you feel too fragile to take on Napoli today.

Nina had said there was also a ferry to Ischia from Pozzuoli, on the outskirts of Naples, so you check a station map and find that the underground goes directly there. You don't even have to venture outside. You buy a ticket and take the rickety metro to Pozzuoli, and then make your way from the subway station down some hairpin stairs, through haphazard stucco houses, all the way to the port. You wander around streets lined with pizza, *gelato,* and clothing shops that look left over from another decade. Eventually you find your way to the tourist office, where you learn that Pozzuoli is mainly an old fishing town, destroyed by earthquakes and hastily rebuilt, it seems, by people who knew it might crumble again anyway. It's famous for being the birthplace of Sophia Loren, and for having an ancient amphitheater, the Anfiteatro Flavio, built in the first century A.D., where it's still possible to see the underground galleries where animals were kept before they were released into the theater to eat whoever had the misfortune of being dinner that day. Everyone in the tourist office is eager to have you spend the night there, to see the sights, and they're disappointed when, like most of the other tourists, you ask only when the next boat leaves for Ischia.

You have some time before the boat departs, so you find a *panino* in one place—how can every small, rundown sandwich shop in Italy have such good tomatoes, bread, and fresh mozzarella?—and a coffee in another. The people you encounter in the bars and shops in Pozzuoli seem like they're from another, more traditional era than those in Florence. You feel self-conscious, out of place, a single American woman in her mid-thirties; it's as if people don't know what to call you. You're certainly old enough to be a signora, and ought to be married. But there you are, traveling solo, with no wedding band. Signorina? You don't fit.

While you're waiting at the port, some little girls, about eight years old, come up to you and circle around. They have sparkling barrettes and scuffed shoes and big brown eyes and want to know if they can have your telephone card for their collection if you're finished with it. You hand it over, even though there are still a few hundred lire left on it, and the girls examine it, squealing in delight. They call you *signora,* because you are older than their mothers. They ask where you are from, and they've never heard of San Francisco, except, of course, for the saint himself. "America," you say, and they're excited. *Americana!* They're full of questions, and wonder where your children are hiding.

"I don't have any children," you tell them, and that puzzles them.

"Where is your husband?" one asks.

"He left," you say, and they are startled by your response, uncomprehending. You look down at your shoes and say, "He died," because that they can understand. They nod solemnly and wave you off to the boat.

There's another ship next to yours, leaving for Tunisia. It's tempting to board that one, to go someplace even more exotic and far away than Ischia, to lose yourself completely and maybe never come back. Who knows who you might happen to encounter in Tunisia. It could change your life. The big upheavals always come from random, chance encounters. Like the night almost five years before, when you met your husband. It had been raining, and you didn't really want to leave the house, but your boyfriend was parked in front of a basketball game, uncommunicative, and so you decided to go to a party by yourself. Sipping a Scotch there, you drifted into the kitchen to add some water to your drink, and ran into a bushy-headed man leaning up against the sink. He gave you a brilliant smile, complimented your hat, and you got to talking, talked about everything, until the party started breaking up. You weren't physically attracted to Jon at first; his head seemed too big for his thin, almost delicate body, and he had long, pale, daddy longlegs fingers. But he was full of excitement, teetering toward manic, talking about books and places, fascinated with you and your work. He had an intense spotlight on you, and you liked the attention. You told him how much you'd enjoyed chatting with him; it was like when you're traveling and you meet someone you know you'll never see again, so you can say anything.

You lost track of him as you were leaving the place, and almost panicked for a moment, until you found him standing under the eaves outside with the rain pelting down, waiting. You exchanged cards, he promised to call, and you made it clear that while you had a boyfriend, you hoped you could be friends. He sent you flowers and a book the next day—irises and Diane Ackerman's *A Natural History of the Senses*—and insisted on seeing you again. You had dinner together, he told you he thought you were beautiful, he said that being friends wasn't enough, and he kissed you good night. He persisted, and then one weekend when your boyfriend was out of town, a dear friend of yours died, and you found yourself seeking Jon for comfort. He listened, he gazed at you with his soulful brown eyes and threw a gangly arm around you while you cried. You went away together, you split up with your boyfriend, you spent a succession of romantic evenings and weekends with him, and he married you two and a half years later. He toasted you then, saying that when he'd met you at the party, and started talking, it was the most startlingly sudden feeling of intimacy he'd ever experienced, and he'd wanted that conversation to go on forever.

You board your boat, the boat to Ischia, and climb to the top deck, where the air is fresh and cool, the sun sinking behind the silhouetted island in the distance. Traveling by boat is romantic, pulling you away from shore, leaving a vast emptiness of water between your old life and an entirely new place. But as the engines warm up and the horn sounds and the ship belches black smoke, you realize you can't outdistance your pain; it hangs in the wet air and covers your face with salt water.

When the boat pulls in to Ischia's crater-round harbor, it's evening. You ask an African man selling baskets and beads from a blanket spread out on the dock where you can find the bus to the island's largest town, Forio. He checks his watch and says he's headed that way, he'll show you, and he gathers up all his stuff into one big zippered gym bag. You aren't so sure at first that you want a guide, but he's friendly and polite, curious about you. He tells you all about the island as he shows you to the bus. He's young, maybe seventeen—still a boy, really—and had left his entire family back in Senegal two years earlier, not sure when he'd see them again. His Italian is perfect, and it's strange to be speaking Italian with a young African man, an odd commonality between people from two different ends of the earth. You mention a Senegalese singer you're crazy about, telling him how when you saw him in concert, he'd conducted the second half sitting on the floor in white robes, the whole audience cross-legged, rapt. The African man brightens at that reminder of home—even though your saying you've heard of a Senegalese singer named Youssou N'dour was a little like him saying he'd heard of an American singer named Bob Dylan.

The bus circles around the island on a winding road, past all kinds of hotels and resorts. You show the African man the different *pensione* listed in your guidebook, and he recommends one, and tells you when to get off at the right stop. "If you have time," he says, waving *ciao*, "go to Sant' Angelo. It's the most beautiful place on the island." You thank him, wish him luck getting back home someday, swing your day pack onto one shoulder, and head out into the street.

In Forio, motorbikes race through the streets, tourist cafés have all-German menus, and souvenir stores sell stuff you'd never dream of hauling home. You hate Forio; it isn't the charming island village you expected, you can't find a good meal anywhere, the red wine is sour, and the only saving grace seems to be the *pensione* the African man recommended, which, when you arrive, looks peaceful and clean with large tropical plants in an open-air stairway.

In the morning, after a pot of coffee and a warm buttered roll, Forio isn't nearly so bad. The signora, like the African man, recommends visiting Sant' Angelo, a smaller village with plenty of beaches, five kilometers away. So you climb aboard a bus filled with German pensioners in mismatching floral shorts and T-shirts and pass several of the thermal baths on Ischia, places that offer all manner of soaking and sweating and rubbing, amusement parks for the arthritic. Finally the bus disgorges the last passengers into a pedestrian-only zone, and noisy, touristy Ischia becomes quiet. You make your way down a narrow street toward the beach, where there is a small piazza with a couple of simple cafés, with outdoor tables that face the little wooden boats bobbing in the water. A slim strip of beach connects the edge of the island to a small, steep volcanic hill, where a few sheep graze. Ischia has turned into the lovely Mediterranean haven you've been dreaming about.

After another coffee, you walk down to the beach and hail a boat taxi that takes you even farther away, past the restaurants with sun umbrellas for rent, to a free pebble beach where you can spread out your big scarf, lie down, and forget the advice of American dermatologists for an entire sunny morning. You cast an eye about the beach and realize that if you were hoping for a fling, you would have to settle for a pot-bellied German pensioner. Never mind. It's a splendid day. From time to time you wade into the clear warm water, thinking about nothing, reveling in the freedom to swim and swim forever in the smooth Italian sea.

Around lunchtime you spot a white building nearby with blue awnings and large palm umbrellas and a terrace on top, where a couple of deeply bronzed people seem to be sunbathing in the all-and-all. You wonder, since the place has no name, if it's a private club or whether you can go sit under one of those nice big umbrellas yourself. You hesitate, but decide, what the hell, you're a Blonde American Divorcée and no one is likely to complain if you tie your sarong around your waist and go sit on his patio and dry your hair in the sun. You walk in, stopping to use the shower on the way, and sit down at one of the tables. The place is nearly empty.

You need hardly have worried about not being welcome. As soon as you sit down an older man at the next table gets up and introduces himself as Nicola, and from the name on the menu—"Da Nicola alle Fumarole"—you gather he's the owner. He asks what you'd like, and you say maybe if there's some lemonade, that would be nice. "Of course," he says, and motions to a waiter. You remark that it's a beautiful place, with its view of the ocean and the jutting rock offshore, and he says, *"È ancora più bello con una bella donna qua."*

The waiter, tall and about forty with classic features, brings you lemonade made from fresh, tart lemons. You notice that the men at the table next to you are eating an arugula salad, and after awhile you realize that what you really need is some of that salad and a piece of good bread and a glass of white wine. As the waiter arrives with his tray, he tells you how nice it is to see a beautiful young woman at the end of the season when there are usually only pensioners around. You are neither quite young nor beautiful, but you're happy to play the part. You know he's just flattering you, as he would any woman who happened to be in his vicinity, but it doesn't matter. Lately, the only people in San Francisco who've called you beautiful have been hoping for some spare change.

The salad is deep green and just slightly bitter against the smooth olive oil, and the wine is so light it might as well be water. After lunch and coffee, the waiter shows you the way to the terrace where Germans are sunning themselves in the nude on lounge chairs. He adjusts a chair until it's nearly flat, pats the seat, and tells you to have a nice nap. Afterward, he says, you can try the sauna and the *fango,* which after some confused description you understand is a mud mask with apparently special radioactive healing powers.

You give yourself over to the waiter's suggestions, starting with the nap, but despite his sober advice that it is healthiest done nude, you keep your swimsuit on. You feel too much like the lone woman on a sun roof full of grizzled, naked men. After a good snooze, you head down the stone stairs to the ocean for a wake-up swim. The waiter sees you getting out of the water, and tells you that you have to have a sauna next, and he shuts you into a wooden room built into the hill, filled with steam that comes hissing straight out of the volcanic earth, scented with fennel. After a few minutes, he knocks on the door, telling you it's time for another dip in the ocean, then a quick shower, and then a *fango.* There is clearly a system going, so you follow his instructions.

After the shower, the waiter shows you the *fango,* a jar of volcanic mud he's collected from hot springs on the island. He expertly slathers it all across your face and shoulders, carefully explaining that you already have such lovely skin that the *fango* will, in your case, only be preventive. He instructs you to leave the mud on to dry and crack in the sun up on the sun roof. You lie down among the nudists again, your face covered with mud, and an Italian whispers, *"Sposa di Frankenstein."* You smile and feel the mud stiffen on your skin. When the *fango* is done, you take another sauna to rub off all the mud, and your skin is in fact unbelievably soft. You race into the ocean for a refreshing swim before coming back to a thermal pool hidden in a deep rock grotto. You ease yourself into the steaming water and close your eyes. When the waiter climbs in and settles down next to you, you begin to dimly realize that he is not doing all of this for a better tip.

He sits with you in the sauna and starts flirting outrageously: your skin is the color of gold, so soft. And your body. What a beautiful body, so nice from so much swimming, so strong, so curvy. *Bella, bella.* Yeah, yeah. He is, of course, saying all the things a Blonde American Divorcée is dying to hear, and in soft Italian. But it's all a bit much, and he doesn't seem to have anything else to say. He rubs the last few bits of mud off your throat and chest, presses himself closer, and then he kisses you, no tentative soft nibbles, just a hard push. Despite how wonderful the whole *fango* regime has been, you're quite sure you don't want to kiss him back. Here he is, the Italian lover you'd fantasized about. He'll be wild about you, he'll make passionate love to you, yet he leaves you absolutely cold. Maybe, you think, as you make excuses and slip away, you just have no desire for men at all anymore.

That evening, over dinner in a simple pizza place, you meet an American woman, Pamela, who has lived on Ischia for thirty years. You wonder what it would be like to leave your home to live on a faraway island, like she has, doing odd translations for money, having tourists stay in your extra rooms, spending years of afternoons in the sun. Maybe it would be great to just chuck it all, have a big yard sale in San Francisco and move to an Italian island for good. But while Pamela seems cheerful on the surface, she is alone after all those years, and it gives her a bitter edge. She has funny but harsh things to say about the islanders, the Germans, and tourists in general.

You get the feeling that even though Pamela craves your company, someone to speak English with, another American, she also resents you somehow. She asks you why you are traveling alone, and you explain that you were recently separated from your husband, and wanted to get away. She asks how old you are.

"Thirty-six," you say, and Pamela peers closer to inspect your face.

"You should lie about your age," she concludes. "You could say you're thirty."

"Why?" you ask. It has never occurred to you to worry about your age. It is what it is.

Pamela gives a hard laugh. "You'll see."

The next day you meet up with Pamela and her friend, an overly gregarious photographer in his forties, who takes you in a '62 Ford sedan to a hidden canyon on the island where mineral water comes pouring down through the rocks in small waterfalls. There is a run-down spa at the mouth of the canyon, and Pamela says the place used to be free, but now you have to wait until the people who run it close down for lunch, and then you sneak in. So you all wait, sunning yourselves on a slope next to the trail, until a woman shouts from a house above that it's time to come to the table, and the man in the ticket booth locks up and leaves. You slip into the baths, keeping an eye out for the people who work there, trying not to make noise splashing. You stand under the pounding hot mineral shower as it melts all the knots in your neck and shoulders. Afterward, you walk back to the beach, drink a couple of beers, and the islanders talk about how much the place has changed over the years, ruined by all the tourists.

Pamela drifts away to chat with a friend on the beach, leaving you alone with the photographer. Right away, he starts telling you how much he's attracted to you. You say he shouldn't be saying things like that with his girlfriend nearby, and he scowls, saying Pamela isn't his girlfriend at all. "Have you seen her body?" he asks. "She is an old bag." He can't be that much younger than she is, and suddenly you understand Pamela's resentment.

Then the photographer asks you why you don't wear a bikini, you'd look great in a bikini. Mediterranean men like women with curves, he says, you should show them all off. You don't wear bikinis for the same reason you wouldn't wear shorts in Paris; you don't want to have to imagine the comments. You tell him you prefer a practical suit for swimming, and with that you push off and out into the sea to get away from him. He swims after you and, treading water, suggests that you should spend the night together. He has some really great music you could listen to. Some Carpenters and some Fleetwood Mac. Plus, he says, he has studied yoga and he knows that your energy would be good together.

You keep on swimming, biding your time in the water until you see Pamela return to her spot on the beach. You get out, thank her for showing you around, and say you're sorry, you have to leave, you have a phone call to make to the States.

The photographer, shaking himself dry like a dog, catches that last part. "You Americans," he says disdainfully, "you are always having to leave to make telephone calls."

You return to Forio alone, sneaking past the restaurant you

ate at the day before so the waiter won't see you. Italian lovers, you realize, are as easy to pick up on Ischia as ceramic ashtrays painted with lemons.

You go back to the *pensione* and sit on the roof terrace and decide it's just fine to be by yourself. You eat a picnic dinner, read a few pages of a novel, and then go to bed, making plans to move on the next day because already the island feels too small.

A mosquito wakes you in the dead of night and you find yourself in tears. You switch on the lamp and write a twelve-page letter to your husband, trying to piece together an explanation for his betrayal, a letter you will never send. But putting it all down in a notebook in a *pensione* on Ischia makes you feel better. In the morning, you are ready to explore someplace new, alone.

{THREE}

SANT' ANGELO

At breakfast you say good morning to the signora and nod to a gentleman at the table next to yours. You notice he isn't German and wonder about him. He looks remarkably like Bob Dylan did ten years before, only less craggy, with shiny brown curls, a beaklike nose, and watery blue eyes. He is wearing a long soft denim jacket and a tapestry vest and a thick silver bracelet. No one joins him at his table; he seems to be alone.

You're studying the pages you ripped out of your guidebook when the man starts asking the signora some questions about the island in Italian. Curious, you join in and ask her something yourself about the hike up the volcano, never making eye contact with the man. But when the signora leaves, you offer him a look through the guidebook chapter on the island. You speak to him in the third person formal, *Lei*. He takes the torn papers from your hands.

"You travel light," he observes in Italian, and glances through the pages.

He doesn't seem to read much English, so you take the pages

33

back and explain what you know about the island from your two days' experience. You chat; he asks how long you've been traveling, and when you're leaving, and you tell him you're probably leaving that morning but you still aren't sure, you might want to climb the dormant volcano first. You find out that he is from Paris, but half-Italian, which is why he speaks the language so well. An art teacher. You ask if he teaches in high school, and he says, no, at a university, a professor.

He asks about you, and you say you're a journalist, freelance, you write for women's magazines, general interest, that sort of thing. He says he first guessed by looking at you that you were German, but your accent is good and he can't tell where you're from. You say you're from San Francisco, which you always say instead of America.

"Ahh," he says, *"San Francisco deve essere una bella città."* It must be a beautiful city. He turns his chair toward you slightly and crosses his legs. *"Sei lontana da casa,"* he says. You're a long way from home. He has slipped into the second person familiar, *tu.* You're just traveling around, you explain, and one of your Italian friends had recommended Ischia. You like stretching the summer out by being in a place where the water is still warm in late September.

"Anch'io," he says. Me too.

Your brain parts company with your mouth for a moment and you tell him he has a face like Bob Dylan. He seems surprised at what a direct and personal thing that is to say, you American you, and you quickly add "ten years ago," though it's probably closer to five, and he doesn't really look displeased. Amused.

"Wasn't it strange," he says, "that Bob Dylan just played for the pope in Bologna? Has he become a Catholic or what? And what's with the hat?"

"It's always hard to know what religious phase Bob Dylan is in," you say. "But the hat was way too cowboy."

"The day the Stones play 'Sympathy for the Devil' for the pope," he says, "I'll become a papist."

You like his sensibility and can't help giving him a smile before returning to your coffee. After a few minutes he mentions that if in fact you do decide to climb the mountain instead of leaving that morning, he'd be pleased to join you, if you'd like the company. You shrug: Why not. Pompeii can wait.

In a few minutes you meet outside the *pensione* and climb aboard a crowded bus. You notice that he, like you, has brought along a beach bag. He leans close to you and asks your name. *"Laura,"* you say, with the pretty rolling Italian pronunciation. He tells you his name and you say, in your best schoolbook Italian, that it is a pleasure to meet him. He holds out his hand to shake, making fun of your formality.

The bus takes you to the highest road on the island and you walk another three kilometers until the road turns into a small brushy footpath and reaches the summit, Mount Epomeo. From there, you really know you're on an island, water on all sides, Capri just obscured by the clouds. You sit on volcanic rocks overlooking everything while he smokes an unfiltered cigarette.

"There's no sight I love more than grapevines with the ocean in the distance," he says. You talk about all the islands you've been to, Stromboli and Sardinia, Crete and Santorini, and find you've both climbed to the top of Formentera, the tiny island off Ibiza. You go further afield and talk about other places you've traveled in the world. You tell him one of your best stories already, about the time you interviewed Yasir Arafat in his villa in Baghdad ten days before the Persian Gulf War—how there were giant paintings of a white stallion on one wall and Saddam Hussein on the other, how unbelievably charismatic Arafat was in person, how all his bodyguards with machine guns jumped when they heard the noise your automatic camera made when it rewound the film. You're eager all of a sudden for this Frenchman to think you're something more than a ditzy American who writes for women's magazines. He's curious but unimpressed, which you like, and the conversation shifts from what the British and Americans are still doing in Iraq to French politics, then to Bill Clinton.

"American politics are ridiculous," he says. "Who cares who the president sleeps with? At least Kennedy had better taste in women."

"We are far too puritanical," you agree, "whatever the woman looks like."

At Mitterand's funeral, he explains, his mistress was right there with his wife. Much more civilized. The problem with Americans, he says, is they think a little affair will destroy a marriage. How can they be so claustrophobic? It puts far too much pressure on the marriage. *That's* what will ruin a marriage.

That, you think, and falling in love with someone else.

A troop of tourists, hiking with boots and walking sticks, arrive at your rock outcropping, so you leave. On the way down the mountain, wandering through little terraced orchards with lemon and fig trees, the professor asks about your marriage. We're just traveling, he says, you can tell me anything. You tell him the story in brief—so in love, married only a year and a half when he left, abruptly, hard to say why, a complicated psychological scenario.

"Did you have time for affairs?" he asks.

"No," you say. "But I think my husband did."

"Well, that is all history. That is all behind you now, yes?"

"Sort of." You continue down the trail for a while, and then you ask him if he is married.

"I'm not talking," he answers, in English.

"That answers the question," you say.

Okay, he says, he's been married for ten years and has two children. You tell him you know better than to ask whether he's had time for any affairs, and he smiles—you're learning fast.

You find yourself wondering whether you would have an affair with a married man, and decide that in the United States, you would not. But you aren't in the United States. You're outside your country, your language, and really, your life. And he—well, he is French. The French are notorious for their extramarital liaisons; as far as you know, it's a way of life. The idea titillates you, but it seems unlikely that you'd have an affair with him anyway. He's too remote, sophisticated, too different from any man you've ever known. You don't even speak the same language. He isn't even flirting with you. He seems to enjoy your company, and that's all, that's nice.

You ask him what a married man is doing traveling by himself on an island in the Mediterranean. He explains that it's understood in his household that, once a year, he needs his solitude. He has to get away from Paris and just sit on an island and *far niente*, do nothing, so that he can be his Mediterranean self for a while. He needs to be able to relax completely, which is impossible to do in Paris. He is part Italian and part Arab, and he has to spend some time being an Oriental man, living where the days are warmer and slower. It's in his blood.

After you make it down the mountain, you find a place for

lunch, which the French professor eats with a precise sense of ritual. You just want a salad, and he says you have what you want, women are always just eating salad, but he's having a real meal. He has a salad, a roast pork *panino,* and then a coffee, and finally he slowly smokes a cigar. When he stubs out the cigar, he suggests a swim.

You mention a beach you've heard about, the Sorceto, where hot water bubbles up from the rocks. You consult his map and find a bus to take you to the far side of the island, and then you walk down a steep trail to the beach. He leads you, taking your hand, stepping gingerly over slippery wet rocks, past some high boulders to the part of the beach away from all the people. After a long swim, you wade in the hot springs, and then lie down on the pebbles for a nap, stretched out next to him.

"So what do you think?" he asks.

You have no idea what to do with that open-ended question. You think you know what he means, but you aren't sure.

"Bel posto," you answer. Lovely spot.

The two of you lie there quietly, soaking up the sun for a while.

He tries again, more direct this time. *"Allora,"* he says. Now then. "What do you think of *me*?"

You know the situation has all the makings of an opening, an exciting opportunity, but you just aren't sure, you're somehow scared. You turn the question around, not about to risk anything. "You tell me, professor," you say. "What do you think of me?"

He weighs his words. *"Una ragazza piacevole."* A pleasant girl, he says, or maybe pleasing, or pleasurable. He makes the word sound like he's just bitten into a ripe peach. "It's a nice coincidence that we met at the *pensione,* no?" he asks. "We seem to be on the same frequency." He taps his temple. "That's rare."

"Umm." You dig into the pebbles and realize the rocks on the beach aren't warmed from the sun but from inside the earth. The farther you dig down into the rocks, the warmer they are. You lie on your stomach and just when you are drifting off you feel a warm, smooth stone placed lightly on the small of your back and all the desire you thought was dead radiates from that rock throughout your entire body. And then his hand touches you where the rock had been and traces soft patterns all the way down to the very bottom of your spine.

In the evening you find the only restaurant in Forio where Italians are eating, and you talk over pesto like old friends. You ask him what classes he teaches, and he mentions art history and the philosophy of aesthetics, and you tell him how terrible it was in college that your modern art history class was held in the morning. "You fell asleep when the lights went out to watch the slides," he says. You nod. "You're lucky you weren't in my class, *cara*."

You didn't do so well as it was, you tell him. You knew so little about art in your freshman year that during the first quiz, when you had to choose any work of modern art to describe, you picked Marcel Duchamp's "The Bride Stripped Bare by Her Bachelors, Even," because you liked the title.

The professor groans. "There have been whole libraries written about that work," he says, "and still no one really understands it." He asks if you failed.

"It was a disaster." You tell him how you went to the professor and explained that you were at a distinct disadvantage, because almost everyone else in your college grew up in New York or on the East Coast and had been exposed to art, going to the Metropolitan and the MOMA with their parents or on prep school field trips. You grew up in Colorado, and so the only art you knew about was Native American art. You know how to tell a good Navajo rug, though.

"Clever argument, *signorina*," he says. "And?"

"He gave me another chance. I picked someone easier, Jackson Pollock."

"Ah." The French professor takes a few bites of pesto, and tells you he is interested in Native American art, since his mother was an academic who wrote about native cultures.

You can see the mention of his mother makes him sad. You ask if his mother is still living, and he says she died many years ago. His father died more recently, only a couple of years ago.

"I'm sorry."

"It is a strange thing, to be an orphan—even at this age, even with a family," he says, allowing a glimpse into his personal world. "You always feel a little bit alone."

You notice he is near tears. He covers up by shifting his tone, gesturing to the waiter to bring a coffee. You tell him you're sorry. You say you're lucky that your parents are still alive and healthy and tell him a little about them.

"Are you friends with them?" he asks.

"Yes," you say. "They're wonderful people."

"So were my parents," he says. He stares into his empty espresso cup. "We're both lucky." He takes your hand and holds it until the check comes.

You leave the restaurant and return to the *pensione* discreetly, at different times, with a plan to meet later. He'd given you his room number. You sit in your room, brushing your hair, vaguely scared. You like him, you feel easy in his company, but you can't just go to his room. You can't even move. You stare at the letter you wrote the night before, spread out on your bedspread, and you pick it up, glance through, crumple it, and throw it in the trash. Then you put your brush down, take your key, and sneak into his room.

He greets you with a bright smile as you sit down on the very edge of his bed. You notice that he is naked under the covers and stare instead at the little wooden cross hung on the wall. You don't know what to do. You aren't prepared for this. All you can think about is what a shame it is that you didn't bring any pretty underwear to the island. You grew up being reminded that you should always wear nice clean underwear in case you have to go to the doctor suddenly, but no one ever said anything about wearing sexy ones in case you run into a French aesthetics professor on an island. You've always been nervous about taking off your clothes anyway. You have a tummy and big thighs and a monumental round ass, although to be fair, there have always been great fans of that ass. You finger the fabric on the edge of the bed.

He opens his arms. "Come here, *signorina*."

You peel off your sandals and stretch out next to him, fully clothed. You lie like that for a while while he strokes your hair and your cheek and then puts one of his fingers in your mouth. He holds your face and kisses it all over, eyelids and cheeks and temples, and then pats the covers on the bed.

"*Vieni*," he says, throwing back the sheets to let you in. You take off your sweater, uncertain, scared, and he reaches up and turns off the light switch. You take off the rest of your clothes and climb under the covers. You like how his body feels, smooth, relaxed, soft, with ropy legs. You press against him and feel his magnetic warmth. He gives you a thousand soft caresses on your back, your ass, your thighs. He slides his hand all the way down your leg and squeezes the arch of your foot, touching your whole body, not just zeroing in on your sexual parts, the way your husband had. You always had the feeling with your husband that he loved you despite your body, and this feels so different.

You will the thought of your husband out of the bed. You feel desired; you feel like your whole being is a sexual organ. You tell him that he has such a sweet touch.

There's a moment of awkwardness when neither of you can quite handle the condom smoothly. "I'm lucky," he says, sighing. "I am the perfect age, to have spent most of my sexual life in that brief period between the Pill and AIDS. But now—" He's at a loss.

"We'll manage."

You cuddle next to him, kissing his temple through his soft hair. You touch him softly until he's hard again, becoming more friendly with the condom, pressing your face close, rubbing him with your cheek and then your mouth.

You guide him inside you, and feel him touch that hungry spot, deep inside; you feel, suddenly, how much you've missed sex. You feel full, and you give him a little squeeze.

After awhile, he reaches over for his box of cigarettes and lights one.

"I am dead," he says. "I am a victim of sex."

He seems so serious you don't know what to think. So you curl up next to him, put one hand lightly on his ribs, and close your eyes, trying to sleep.

In the morning, you get up before he is awake, quietly gather your clothes and put them on, then tiptoe from his room to yours around the open stairway. The eagle-eyed signora in the courtyard below catches you walking where you have no business walking and you realize you'd better leave the *pensione* that morning.

You shower and dress, putting on the only other shirt and underwear you brought with you. You pack your few things in the day pack and have no idea what will happen today. You think about leaving, taking an early boat off the island, and never seeing him again. If it was just a quick one-night stand—and how could it be anything else?—you want to be the one to leave first.

But there is no going anywhere without coffee and breakfast, no matter what drama is going on, so you decide to face the morning and the signora. You're nervous walking down to the dining room, and relieved to see that there's already a table of boisterous Germans there, and that it's the signora's daughter who is serving breakfast. You sit down and are grateful when the young woman brings you one ceramic pitcher of coffee and another of warm milk, along with a basket of rolls.

You're halfway through a buttered roll when the professor enters the room, wearing a fresh, sea-blue cotton shirt. You stop chewing. The signora's daughter shows the professor to his table, the same one as yesterday, next to yours. *"Buon giorno,"* he says to her. He looks at your table and nods to you. *"Buon giorno, signora,"* he says in the same formal, distant voice. You're cringing inside, certain your face is flushed. He sits down and says nothing while the young woman brings him coffee and clears away some things from the Germans' table. He doesn't so much as glance your way, and you feel something in your stomach go cold. When the signora's daughter goes back to the kitchen, he turns toward your table.

"Did you sleep well, *signorina?*" he asks. "You left early."

"I slept pretty well," you say, noncommittally. "And you?"

"Very well," he says, his deep voice still full of sex. "I'm hungry."

The older signora comes in with his coffee, and he greets her. The signora doesn't even look your way. As long as she is in the room, the professor doesn't say a word to you.

"And today, my dear?" he asks easily, after the signora leaves. "What is the plan today?"

"I don't know," you say. "I don't think I can stay on at this *pensione.* The signora saw me coming from your room this morning."

He considers that. "I think she has seen this kind of thing before, on a romantic Mediterranean island."

"I don't feel comfortable," you say. "She thinks I'm a *puttana.*"

He sighs. "It's such a charming place."

"I know," you say. "Maybe I'll go to Procida." Your guidebook, you tell him, says that Procida is a nearby tranquil fishing island, and it might be possible to escape the German tourists there.

The professor is game. "Why not Procida?"

After you each go back to your rooms, pay your bills, and retrieve your passports, you take a crowded bus to the port, and then board a boat to Procida. On the boat you take out your disposable camera and snap a shot of the island as you leave, not sure you'll ever return. You turn to the professor. "May I take one of the French aesthetics professor?" you ask, and he nods, inhaling his cigarette, not about to smile for the camera.

The boat lands on Procida, which is charming in its 1950s neorealist Italian movie style, but the beaches are dirty and deserted and the whole place is simply glum. You start feeling guilty that you have taken the professor away from paradise and that you've spent half a day of vacation on crowded buses and a boat, having no idea where you're going. You finally get off the bus and walk toward a *pensione* listed in the guidebook, asking the locals for directions after it seems like you've walked for miles. At last, you find the *pensione,* a rundown place with a tropical profusion of plants, but there is no one there except an eleven-year-old girl looking after a baby, so you decide to wait until after lunch to check in. You have to take a bus all the way back to the port to find a restaurant, which ends up having wonderful food, *pasta allo scoglio,* with mussels, clams, tiny snails, olive oil and parsley, in itself worth the visit, and that puts you back in a cheerful mood. After lunch, the boat back to Ischia seems a lot more appealing than staying on the island.

"Procida," the professor pronounces. *"Non è un gran che."* It isn't a big deal. He suggests going back to the same *pensione* in Forio, which he liked, but you say you really didn't feel comfortable there. You suggest Sant' Angelo instead, and by evening you are back to the whitewashed village with the bright geraniums and fragrant jasmine and oleander. You are hot and tired after another crowded bus ride, but still in fairly good traveling spirits. But after the first hotel you try says it's full, and then the second one does, too, you're defeated. As a last resort you ask if there might be a private room to let somewhere nearby, and the girl at the desk makes a flurry of phone calls. Miraculously, there is a room, with a terrace overlooking the sea, and meals are included at the hotel restaurant. You've found an incredible spot, and it's a good deal. You drop your things in the room and rush down to the beach to jump in.

"Lava tutto," the professor says when his head surfaces. The feeling of the water washes away the whole day.

Afterward, in the room, he arranges his things in tidy piles, his boxes of cigarettes in one spot, his tin of cigars in another. Not sure what to do with yourself, you mention that it's strange to share a room, it's somehow much more intimate than making love. He nods.

"We've made a grand progression in a short time," he says, and then he picks up a big white towel and offers to dry your hair. A little later he thinks you're asleep and he traces his fingers down the curve of your back and then stops. You desperately try to come up with the right verb tenses. Imperfect subjunctive: "If you were to stop touching me," and then present conditional, "I couldn't stand it."

Dinner is on the restaurant terrace, high above the ocean, tiny fishing boats far below. Pino Daniele is playing, southern Italian blues, in the background. There is grilled eggplant and roasted potatoes with rosemary and tomato salad and bruschetta, and that's just to start. Over a piece of lemon-sautéed sole he looks out over the view, the sun sinking red into the ocean, and starts laughing at his luck. "We have found the perfect place," he says.

"Gorgeous," you say in English, and he likes that word, tasting it like wine.

The next day you stretch out on lava rocks away from all the people as the sun washes over you. The professor swims nude and assures you that it is the only way to really enjoy a swim. You take off your swimsuit, dive in, and almost immediately a boat filled with vacationers rounds the corner toward your cove, and you have to hide behind the rocks while the professor, safely back in his shorts, enjoys your predicament.

When you finally come back to your perch he asks if you think he's become more tan in the past two days. There's no discernible difference, but you assure him that he's much more bronze. "Good," he says. "When I return, I want all of the other professors to be jealous."

"They'll be jealous," you say, registering his vanity.

He studies his body. "I could stand to lose a few kilos, too," he says.

The professor is thin, with only a hint of love handles.

"I feel elegant when I am thin," he says, noting your disbelief. "It's more aesthetic."

All this talk about weight suddenly makes you feel self-conscious. "I don't know if that's an absolute aesthetic," you say. "But I guess I could lose a few kilos, too."

He studies your body, as if he were seeing it for the first time. "Yes," he says. "You would be prettier if you were thinner."

That stings. Probably, you think, he really has no desire for you at all. He's just fucking you because there isn't anyone better around. You should just put on your things and leave. You reach for your towel.

But you pause for a second. You realize that if he really didn't desire you, he wouldn't be there. He wouldn't touch you the way he touches you.

"Maybe that's true," you tell him. "But I have a long story with my weight, and if I worry about it, I become neurotic. So I'd rather eat with pleasure and have a few extra kilos."

"Well," he says nonchalantly, "you are a very *sportif* type. This must be right for you."

You relax and talk lazily about authors and films, Marcel Proust and Marguerite Duras, Martin Scorsese, Guy Debord, and *The Night of the Hunter*. The names and titles are a shorthand for what you can't express in your incomplete Italian, but it is enough. You are drugged with pleasure lying on the rocks. It seems like you go through cycle after cycle of swimming, drying off, eating, making love, swimming, and drying off again.

The next morning you ask him what you should do that day and he says, "The same thing we did yesterday. In reverse."

You have an espresso down at the café by the boat taxis and read the Italian newspaper. The professor watches two young teenage girls turning cartwheels in the sand. "Sometimes," he says, "I feel like Humbert Humbert."

You tell him he's terrible, and he says, no, he's just being honest. That's why, he says, *Lolita* is one of the best books ever written, because it's honest. He says he would never dream of trying to seduce a young girl, but sometimes they remind him of his first love, who changed how he felt about himself, and helped him become a man. He had been a beautiful toddler with golden curls, he says, always receiving praise from strangers. But then his nose started to grow. He remembers how his mother even cried once at how her beautiful boy had developed such a monstrous nose. He felt he was ugly until he met a girl from Norway, just his age, fourteen or fifteen, and they fell in love for a summer, even though they barely spoke the same languages. There will never be anything like the sweetness of that first love, he says, or the sorrow of her leaving when she went back to Norway, knowing they would never see each other again, which they never did. But a few weeks after she left, he received a beautiful card she had made, and when he opened it, all it said was, "I love your nose."

You tell him you think the Norwegian girl was right. He has a magnificent Mediterranean nose.

"Thank you, my dear," he says, in English.

At some point it occurs to you that these four days with the professor are unique, that their particular beauty could never be repeated, and that probably you will never see him again. And you realize you might never have another lover like him, either. His lovemaking is like a long, languorous meal, full of delightful appetizers and side dishes, a variety of simple, exquisite tastes, finished off by an unfiltered cigarette.

"After thirty-six years you decide to take up smoking now?" he asks. You smile and tell him it's all his fault.

"When I get back," you say, "I'm going to have to find a lover like you."

"Inutile," he says, and laughs. Your only hope is to teach someone, he says. Then he becomes more serious, avuncular. "You'll find someone," he says. "All you need is a man who is older than you and younger than me. A professor of literature who speaks Italian. There must be some of them in San Francisco."

"They're everywhere," you say, "like German tourists."

On your last evening before leaving, the weather turns cold, it's fall already. You change from your swimsuit and sarong into the same worn black jeans, black T-shirt, and black sweater that you've been wearing now for days. Your bra is dirty, so you go without, and you haven't brought a belt, so your pants are slipping down. The professor always wears a perfectly pressed, fresh shirt with his jeans. You're a mess, and apologize that you don't have anything nice.

He doesn't seem to care. He looks at you. "You must be cold." He offers you one of the woven scarves he's brought along. You thank him, but tell him you would really prefer the blue one he's wearing, it would look better on you. He says he can see you have the instinct to dress up when you want to and reluctantly unwinds the scarf from his neck, telling you it's his favorite, he got it in Egypt. You like it. It spruces up everything, and secretly wish he would give it to you as a present to remember him by.

Over dinner, he's quiet. He asks you a couple of questions about your husband, what he's like, and you tell him he's extremely intelligent, and just as psychologically complicated. The two always seem to go together.

He says that he himself is not complicated at all. "I'm a simple person," he says. "I like art, I like women, I like the sea, good food, cigars." He unwraps the cellophane on a cigar and lights it. "I like pleasure," he says. He smokes quietly for a moment. "Sometimes," he says, "my wife thinks I'm too simple."

You wonder about his wife. You suppose they must have an arrangement—he is traveling alone, and this is hardly his first affair. Whatever there was between them, you were not the problem.

You tell the professor you've never met an intellectual like him who is so uncomplicated, who seems to have no hidden dark corners in his psyche, though you suspect there are a few he isn't talking about. He's so comfortable with himself, seemingly so content with his life. Unlike many of the talented, intelligent men you've run into, he isn't arrogant on the surface with deep insecurities lurking just beneath. He doesn't seem like he'd ever be threatened by strong, smart women, just amused. He's easily delighted, and relaxing to be around. You're glad at least to have a glimpse of that type of man.

You shift your gaze to the candle at the table, and see it reflected in your glass. "You know what I love?" you say. He looks expectantly. "I love this grappa. It smells like the very essence of grapes, down to the soil."

He watches you. "You know, for an American, you aren't so bad."

You take another little sip. "For a Parisian," you say, "neither are you."

You look out at the sea. You're leaving the next morning, you have to go back to the city you shared with your husband. You're quiet for a while. You ask the professor if he was thinking about school on Tuesday and he says no, he was thinking about you.

"Cara signorina," he says, his only compliment. You dear woman. "In such a short time, you know me better than most people do." That seems surprising; surely such a charming man has a lot of friends. You feel like you scarcely know him at all. Then he chuckles slightly. "You know about my secret life. You *are* my secret life."

You don't say anything. You just keep looking at your glass.

"Maybe," he says, "we will find each other again sometime."

"I hope so," you say, concentrating on watching the ship lights in the distance. You look back at him. "You really should see San Francisco someday," you say.

He puffs on his cigar and nods.

The next morning is all business. You pack your few things, and give him back his scarf. You exchange addresses, and he writes down the names of an author and a video artist he'd spoken about, Thomas Bernhard and Bill Viola. He disappears for a few minutes, and comes back with a present for you, a little package of salted capers from the island. You take a bus ride to the port, buy your tickets, find a café with a kiosk and read your separate papers—*Le Monde* and the *International Herald Tribune*—in silence. You board the ship to Naples where you practice putting distance between each other.

In Naples, he helps you find the train station and your ticket and then takes you to a very quick, noisy Napolitano lunch. You have barely finished your *insalata caprese*—fresh tomatoes, buffalo mozzarella, and basil drizzled with olive oil—when he seems anxious to leave. He pays for lunch, and leads you across the street to the train station. He points out the track number and tells you to send him a postcard at Christmas.

Then he abruptly says, "I'm abandoning you here," and kisses you lightly, once on each cheek, *ciao, ciao.*

"Piacere," you murmur, a pleasure, and he is gone.

You board the train and stand in the corridor, stunned. It was such a quick good-bye, such a quick four days, a dream. But even though he's gone, and you know you'll never see him again, you feel lighter somehow.

You don't even bother looking for a seat until the train lurches out of the station and you nearly fall. Then you go from car to car and find that everything is full, even the jump seats in the hall. Finally you reach the cafeteria car and decide to just sit down at a table there. You try to collect your thoughts when you hear someone call your name. It must be another Laura, Italy is full of Lauras, but then you hear it again, closer. An absurd hope leaps through your mind that it is the professor, who has decided to follow you anywhere.

You turn and there's the Italian photographer from the second day in Ischia, which seems like months and months ago. He greets you effusively and sits right down across from you. He's the last person you want to see right now, and you can barely stand to speak to him.

"Laura, Laura," he says, "How funny to run into you here! It must be fate."

"Ciao," you smile weakly, willing him to go away. But there is nowhere else for him to sit, and you can't make him leave.

He asks what you are drinking, and you say nothing, thank you. He says he is having lunch, why don't you have something, and you say no, no, you just ate in Naples. It is beyond you how someone could eat in the train pulling out of Naples, when Naples has arguably the best lunch food in the entire world.

"Something to drink, then," he says. He goes to the counter and comes back with a plastic-wrapped sandwich, two plastic cups, and four airplane-sized bottles of white wine. You are stuck with him, so you figure you might as well drink.

He pours and starts chattering about his trip to Rome, where he is shooting photos for postcards—the Coliseum, the Pantheon, the Spanish Steps. How is it possible that there aren't already enough postcards in the world of those places, you wonder, and why does this photographer have to be on this train. You stare out the window while he speaks, and vaguely hear him suggesting that you ought to get out in Rome with him, he could show you around. You drink more of the wine until the alcohol settles in. You want to be alone with your thoughts, with the professor.

Finally the train stops and a few people get out. "I'm so tired," you tell the photographer. "You'll have to excuse me. I need to find a seat." You thank him for the drink, and say goodbye before he can reply. You find a compartment where someone has vacated a seat, and sit down. There is an older Italian couple there, a stern widow, and two Italian professional women. You nod your greetings and close your eyes. The images come swirling before you, the rocks, the terrace, the *pensione,* his kiss good-bye.

"Laura," you hear, and you open an eye to see that the photographer is at the door to the coach. "Laura, I found some seats." The others in the coach jolt awake at his voice and look inquiringly.

"*Grazie, signore,* but I'm fine here," you say.

"Come on, there are seats," he insists.

You glance around the compartment with a concerned look, hoping for reinforcement. They silently give it to you, glaring at the photographer.

"Please," you say, more firmly, formally. "You're very kind, but I'm fine right here." You cross your arms and close your eyes. When you open them again, the train is just pulling out of Rome.

{FOUR}

MILANO

Back home in San Francisco, you keep seeing his face. It pops up in your dreams and hovers in front of your computer screen when you are working: There are his thick dark curls and Egyptian nose, his skin warmly brown from the Mediterranean sun. The Ischia sun. You pause to savor the memory of his rough cheek pressed against your smooth one, his quick kiss good-bye, his figure disappearing into the busy streets outside the train station in Naples.

He is gone, but he sustains you with a sense of possibility, of pleasure. You may be freshly separated from your husband, you may be sleeping alone, and you may figure that your chances of finding a wonderful single man to date in San Francisco are about the same as there being another big earthquake here (it could happen, but you don't really believe it—and, face it, you aren't prepared for it). But somewhere in the back of your mind is that face, that desire, and that island. It keeps lifting you back to buoyancy, even if you don't expect to see or hear from the French professor you met on Ischia ever again.

Then one day a postcard arrives from Paris, a colorful Matisse print of a woman dancing. "It was great!" he writes. "I can't forget . . . Love, M." It is a little treasure you look at too often in the next few weeks. You consider writing back, hoping that his wife doesn't open his mail. Then you think that maybe it would be better not to write, better to leave that perfect fantasy, those four splendid days together, alone. And so you don't.

A month or so later, you are packing a bag for a business trip and find the throwaway camera you took with you to Naples in one of the zippered pockets. You'd forgotten about it. You have it developed, and there is the postcard sunset, there is the view from the terrace of the lemon trees and whitewashed houses trailing down to the beach, there is Ischia from the boat, and there is the French aesthetics professor himself, leaning back in sunglasses against the white railing of the ship, flawless blue sky and sea behind him, collar open, tan, cigarette clasped in his smirking mouth. You can't resist.

So you enclose some of the photos in a plain envelope with no return address and mail it off to Paris. You write in Italian that before you went to Ischia, you had a fantasy about encountering a lovely man for a little fling. The reality was so much better than the fantasy, you say, that now you have a much richer imagination. You remember his astrological sign and wish him a happy birthday, too.

A few weeks go by, and you don't hear back. Christmas comes, a crisp, clear day you spend with friends who invite you for brunch and a long walk on the beach with their beagles. You are grateful for your friends, who remember that while the crisis stage of your divorce is over, the drama is spent, and you are no longer falling to pieces over the phone, you are still alone. They check up on you, without being obvious about it, and make sure you have plenty of invitations. Other friends are more uncomfortable with you, as if your bad luck might rub off on them, and stop inviting you to couples-only dinner parties. Your husband's entire group of friends has vanished, like he did; one wrote you a note saying she was sorry, but you've never seen any of them again.

As January approaches, you decide you need to somehow celebrate the year, The Year My Husband Left Me, as finally being over. You want to pronounce yourself single so you can move on. You call up some friends who live in Nevada, up against the eastern Sierras, on what used to be a divorce ranch back in the forties. Swanky East Coast women—Mary Pickford, Rita Hayworth, and Gloria Vanderbilt among them—would take the train to Reno to stay at those divorce ranches for six weeks, riding horses, gambling, lounging by the pool, and flirting with the cowboys. It was long enough to establish residency in Nevada for a quick divorce, and a lot less grueling than proving adultery or mental cruelty. Clare Boothe Luce, who wrote George Cukor's 1939 film *The Women,* stayed for a while at the ranch up the road a piece from where your friends live.

You go to visit, share home-cooked meals with your friends, and play raucous music with them, jamming on three-chord Neil Young songs until all hours on New Year's Eve. The next day you sit in their mom's kitchen, with its wide windows framing the sagebrush plains, and watch Maya make bread while you talk about local politics. The last time you visited these friends, you'd been with your husband, but he'd been anxious to leave early. He always wanted you to himself.

Later on New Year's Day you take a walk around the old divorce ranch, crunching a path in the snow, circling around the individual cabins and the dining lodge made out of hand-hewn logs. You think about all those women who took the train out here to grieve or to whoop it up with the cowboys, the Joan Fontaine and Rosalind Russell types, and you realize that the worst of your sorrow is over. You still cry occasionally, the tears hitting you unaware, and you still feel alone in the evenings, with no one to cook for and no one to talk to about the novel you are in the middle of reading. And as angry as you were at your husband, you still miss him sometimes.

But you're better. You've managed to surround yourself with lively-minded people. Instead of living and working alone in your flat, you did the more complicated thing, and found a roommate and an office outside your house with a group of fellow freelancers. You went back to Colorado for a while, to visit your family and your best friend since fourth grade, who took you on a road trip in the mountains, where everything—her friendship, the landscape—seemed as permanent and unchanging as granite, your marriage just a temporary episode, small in the greater scheme of things. Back at home, you've been determined to keep busy with work, piano lessons, Italian classes, yoga, films, drinks, museum exhibits, all the things that a city like San Francisco has to offer someone who doesn't want to be alone in the evening. You still don't feel like you're much fun to be around; you don't like the pessimistic person who's been inhabiting your body since your husband left. But the worst of the divorce, the serious depression, is behind you. Or at least now you're in the up-and-about phase, like walking pneumonia.

It's strange: you never dreamed that you would ever use the word "depression" with yourself. You always thought, naively, that it was something for sad, maybe even weak people, people who couldn't just pick themselves up, for God's sake, and move on. You didn't realize that it was a leaden presence that came to call, uninvited, and couldn't be driven away with any amount of food, wine, dancing, hiking, or trips to the shrink. It just stayed and stayed until it wanted to leave of its own accord. A few fantasy days on an island had held it at bay for a while, but it had returned shortly after, punishing you for your absence.

But time has helped, and now, four months later, the depression has lifted some. You are starting to imagine a time when you'll be able to think that what was an ending could also be a beginning.

You stand there for a while in the pines, and think about your wedding, everyone gathered casually in a grove of huge redwood trees, sunshine spilling through, a jazz combo playing, some friends coming forward to read poetry, family members welcoming the new bride or groom, your father-in-law the famous philosopher reading something having to do with Mammon and world revolution that absolutely no one understood. Your husband and you recited hopeful poems to each other, made promises, and when the neighbors' two-year-old boy dashed up to the altar to be the center of attention himself, your new husband just scooped him up in his arms, continuing on with the ceremony. Everyone said it was the quirkiest, most beautiful wedding they could remember. When it came time for the mail-order minister in her big floppy sun hat to pronounce you married, she produced a giant sparkly purple wand and waved it around, touching you on your heads. "Shazaam," she'd said. "You're married."

Everyone gave extremely long but entertaining toasts, ate a salmon dinner, and danced under the redwoods until early in the morning. You wandered around in the woods, drank, chatted with friends, and soaked in the hot tub under the stars, everything magic.

Shazaam, you repeat to yourself on the divorce ranch, undoing the spell. You look around to see if there's anyone within earshot, but you are alone. You say it once again for good measure. "Shazaam."

And so you are divorced. Your impromptu divorce ceremony wasn't legal, of course, but, as your husband once put it, before he decided to marry you, who needs a piece of paper from City Hall?

You go home after the New Year and find that while you have in fact turned a little corner with yourself, the legal part of the divorce isn't quite so easy. There are papers to be filed with courts, agreements to be reached, lawyers to talk to. There are mediation sessions with your ex, which leave you feeling depressed and exhausted. You have to use all your wits against Jon, now an adversary, a brilliant lawyer who knows your vulnerabilities better than anyone. You have to harden your heart and go to meetings where you coldly negotiate about money.

It seems—to you, anyway, because Jon certainly has his own story—that he gets it all: his wealth, his house, his new relationship, time to have a family, self-possession, the law on his side. You just get the grim satisfaction of knowing you've been wronged. He married you, promising to share everything for life, wanting to have children, thinking about moving to a place in the nearby hills with some land where the schools were good. And then he left, saying it turned out he just didn't love you after all, let's go our separate ways, no harm done. He never even said he was sorry.

So you find yourself in mediation having to practically beg for scraps of his generosity after arguing and guilt-tripping don't work. You've never depended on your husband in any material way, but during the time you lived with him, thinking it was forever, San Francisco housing prices boomed way out of your reach, leaving you in a permanent state of insecurity. In a court of law, Jon reminds you, and your $350-an-hour lawyer confirms, you'd end up with only a few thousand dollars, and that's before legal fees. In other words, you would get almost nothing. Anything more than that is generous, and the fact that he is wealthy and he left you, lying, for another woman is just your tough luck.

You drive to the mediation office for the final session, and when your husband comes in, he stiffens, a lawyer, a shark, the person you once trusted more than anyone else in the world, and gives you a cool hello. Just then you come up with a plan. "Hey," you say to him, friendly, as if you were telling him the news of the day, as always. "Guess what?"

He is caught off guard. "What?"

"I'm *so* excited," you say. "It's a little thing, but I wanted to tell you because you're the only one I know who'd appreciate it." You beam, delighted. "I did a *handstand* in my yoga class this week!"

"Wow, that's great," he says, giving you that humane, dazzling smile of his. "I didn't even know you were taking yoga." He relaxes completely. You can't argue against Jon the brilliant lawyer, so you've successfully turned him into Jon the yogi, Jon the Grateful Deadhead, Jon the peacenik, who has to abide by the rules of fairness and community, not self-interest and the law.

You lied about the handstand as a strategy, and it worked. Your husband's ultimatum dissolves, you speak calmly about his concerns, and you end up with a bigger settlement than he'd offered—which, while hardly fair in your mind, is at least more than he wanted to pay. And you're done, you'll never have to sit in a room negotiating with him again. You might never have to see him again, period.

As you go about getting your house and your new life in order, you have to face facts. It's difficult to go from having a wealthy husband in a gorgeous house to renting a flat with a roommate again, swooping down several socioeconomic levels at once. But people are kind to you. When you buy a bed, and tell the salesman at an old San Francisco family-owned store that you need it sooner than the usual six weeks, he asks you why. You explain you broke up with your husband, and since the bed was his to begin with (you'd sold most of your furniture when you moved in), he'd taken it with him. "Honey," the salesman says, with a look of disbelief, "we'll have it to you in three days." One friend comes and plays handyman in your flat, wiring light fixtures and hanging shelves. Others loan you furniture. Your roommate helps you completely clean, grout, spackle, roach-proof, and repaint the flat, making it cheerful and new. When it's finished, you open a bottle of good champagne.

You have always taken care of yourself, you've never depended on your husband, and your cozy flat feels like home in a way his place never did. Your roommate is rarely home, and the flat is big, so you can live as you please. You can walk in and play the piano anytime you like, without feeling embarrassed, knowing you're aggravating someone who is making too much of an effort to tolerate the noise. You can play for pleasure, and the little boy next door, now five, the one who ran up front at your wedding, can ring the bell and ask if he can come bang on the drums with you. You put up the art you like, and paint the kitchen bold Tuscan colors. You make whatever food you desire for dinner, set the table for yourself, and never eat in front of the television, as Jon had. You can invite your friends over for dinner anytime (he always hated having company), you can stay up as late as you want, and your neighbors can just drop by. Your home is more comfortable, and you feel increasingly more like yourself being there.

Still, it's hard to come home sometimes, especially that evening after mediation. You know you're going to be alone all evening, all year, who knows how long, while your ex goes back to his new home, where he's already moved in with his girlfriend.

But on the doorstep is a little package waiting for you, from France. You unwrap it and find a battered tin of Gitanes cigarettes, the type you stole from the professor after dinner in Ischia. There is no note, nothing else. You walk up the stairs to your flat, sit at the little breakfast table overlooking the garden two flights below, open the window, and smoke, which you've hardly ever done. The terrible day dissipates in the pleasurable haze of memory.

You realize that it is dangerous to rely on the French professor to cheer yourself up. You try to hold on to the image of him only to remind yourself that there are men out there who are relaxed and romantic, who make you feel like a woman. There don't seem to be any men like that in San Francisco, at least you haven't met any in the many months that you've now been single. But you don't want to become a cliché—a bitter divorced woman, sexually frustrated, anxious to have kids before it's too late, angry that all the men your age are interested only in younger women, worried about crow's-feet and considering cosmetic surgery. And so you hold on to that cheerful hope. There are men like that out there. Somewhere.

You are thinking about all that again one evening, having another one of the professor's cigarettes, when a tiny folded tissue paper flutters out of the tin. "Your letter arrived exactly on my birthday," the professor writes. "Better that these photos exist, because otherwise I couldn't believe it was all real. Today, under cold, gray Parisian skies, *penso con piacere al piacere.* I'm thinking with pleasure about pleasure."

You send him a postcard of the Victorian houses in your neighborhood, and he writes back, saying how it gave him so much desire to visit you. You exchange cards every month or so, and each time you see the French postmark and his continental script, you are excited. Each card is a romantic gift, a quick vacation, a subtly sexy joke. By spring he is suggesting a little rendezvous somewhere between Paris and San Francisco. You tell him that the aesthetic choice would be to never see him again, to keep the memory of your perfect chance meeting intact. He writes back that as an art professor, he likes your argument very much, but as a man he wants to know, What are you doing in September? You write that the only place smack in the middle of Paris and San Francisco is Newfoundland, and that would be a little brisk for sunbathing, no?

In May, a year after your husband left you, a friend announces at a dinner party that she has rented a place in Florence for a month and her friends are invited. It would be nice, you think, to go to Italy for a few days just to flirt. Italian men, unlike American men, like to flirt even when there's no chance of any tangible outcome. They just like to let you know, in restaurants and on the street, that they appreciate women, all kinds of women, that in fact they like women better than anything else in the world, and thank God He made creatures like you.

By contrast most of the American men you've met have more of a museum gift shop mentality about women: What's the point of spending time just appreciating the art if you can't take it home with you? Either they want to sleep with you, and they open doors and pay for meals and do all that, or they don't, in which case you hardly exist any more as a woman—you become a buddy or a business associate, a kind of honorary man.

So you hope the dinner party friend was serious, and you find a cheap flight and book a ticket to Italy. It seems rash, and you can't really afford it, but you think that traveling where people flirt—the shopkeepers, the waiters, even the photographers on the beach—will help you stop feeling so invisible. As an after-thought you scrawl a postcard to the professor telling him when you'll be in Italy. You know he's teaching and has a family and won't be able to get away. But you want him to know that you're thinking of him.

Your phone rings one evening and someone sounding like Gérard Depardieu in *Green Card* asks, "Is it Laura?" You are so surprised you can hardly respond. He asks if he is disturbing you, and you say of course not. You are happy to hear his voice. He tells you what a sweet voice you have on the phone, almost like a child's. Then he is abrupt: When does your plane arrive in Milano? You give him the details. "I'll meet you on the steps of the Duomo at ten o'clock," he says. "I'll wait for you."

On the endless flight to Milano you read a fat book, *The Decameron,* to calm your nerves. Written in the shadow of the 1348 plague, Giovanni Boccaccio's comic masterpiece tells the story of a group of ten upper-crust young women and men who gather in villas outside Florence to wait out the Black Death by dancing, eating, playing music, and telling tales. For ten days they each tell a story on such themes as deception, adultery, misfortunes that end in happiness, loves that end in tragedy, tricks that men and women are forever playing on each other, and getting out of difficult situations with a witty remark. In the midst of death, fear, and sorrow, they live in the moment with as much pleasure as possible.

The stories celebrate luscious sensuality above all else. There is the tale of a judge's wife, for instance, who quickly tires of her husband's feeble sexual appetites (he tries drinking Vernaccia wine for its uplifting properties, to little effect). Kidnapped by a handsome young rogue, she pretends not to recognize her husband when he comes to rescue her. "I would never go back to you," she says when she finally lets on that she knows him, "because if you were to be squeezed from head to toe there wouldn't be a thimbleful of sauce to show for it."

The *Decameron* tales describe the endless varieties of love—adulterous passion, courtly love, enduring marriages, homosexual love, forbidden love, infatuation. The moral—if you can call it that, and why not—is that finding pleasure is more important than any of the constraints society might put on people's inclinations to "forgather" together. As one storyteller comments after a tale of adultery, "And by proceeding with the greatest of discretion, they enjoyed their love together on many a later occasion. May God grant that you enjoy yours likewise."

This, you think, is what Italians read in school instead of *The Scarlet Letter*. No wonder they're better at flirting.

You wonder about the varieties of love, you who have been so hurt by your husband's affair and a divorce, you who are about to spend a weekend with a married man. Is it possible for couples to have affections on the side that don't erode their marriages? When your husband was first spending time with his old high school girlfriend, you were willing to understand, to say it's something that just happens, though not usually in the first two years of a marriage. He was having an affair, but, ever the lawyer, held on to the Clintonesque technicality that in fact he was not, that his penis had not actually entered his girlfriend's vagina, so he hadn't actually cheated. As if giving you that painful detail made him faithful.

Maybe it's different in other cultures, where marriage is less disposable. Maybe it's different if there is a silent understanding that people are human, that one person can't fulfill all your needs for life, where both partners are discreet enough never to hurt the other with information they could happily live without. You wonder if it would be possible to sustain a little fling on the side, one that clearly did not threaten your marriage. Or would someone always be hurt? Are you making life more painful for a French woman you know nothing about except that she likes to read Thackeray and dresses well?

You wonder, too, if you'll be able to see the saucy French professor again without ruining the first brief romance, without some part of yourself falling in love, and inevitably being disappointed.

When you can't read any more, you chat with the Milanese businessman in the seat next to you who, once you land, offers to take you to the center of town with his friend. You accept, partly because you're worried that taking the bus will make you terribly late. You lurch and squeal through morning rush-hour traffic until you finally reach a bar a block from the Duomo. It's 10:15 and they ask you to have a coffee. They have been so kind, and gone so far out of their way, that it is impossible to refuse. You drink your cappuccino and watch the clock hands move closer to 11:00. Finally you exchange addresses in case they ever come to San Francisco, and they show you to the Duomo, waving *ciao ciao*.

You roll your suitcase along the cobblestones and scan the faces of the young people sitting on the steps of the enormous cathedral. You don't see him. You panic: you're late, and you have no backup plan. There's no way to reach him. You sit on the steps and wait, fuzzy from the sleepless flight, anxiously glancing in all directions. You have no idea what to do. There you are in Milano, the ugliest, most unfriendly city in Italy, under thick threatening skies: you don't know where he is, and you have no place to stay. Maybe he's left already. Maybe he missed his train. Maybe he just decided not to come and didn't even bother to say so. You worry that even if he does show up, Milan isn't romantic enough anyway. Nothing could compare to the time you spent on Ischia. It'll spoil everything. You consider leaving, taking a train to Bologna to visit your friend Giovanna.

You get up and wander toward the doors of the cathedral, peeking inside, then turn around and spot a man in a denim jacket with curls touching the nape of his neck. It's the professor. He's perched on the steps, with an empty space beside him. You quietly sit down next to him and he doesn't see you. You press your skin ever so slightly against him and there is a little *frisson* before he turns. *"Ciao,"* you say, and he smiles in an excited way the French rarely allow themselves to smile, and then he takes you in his arms.

"I never dreamed I'd see you again so soon," he says. You look at him and don't know what to say. You never imagined you would really see him again, either, and now here he is and you don't know what to do. He's practically a stranger, you don't speak his language, and yet here you are, you've traveled six thousand miles on the mere chance that he would meet you.

"It's funny, isn't it?" you say. You turn your attention to fiddling with your bag. You have no idea what you're going to do or say.

He tells you, appreciatively, that you look the same, and you tell him he does, too, but in truth he looks much skinnier and more haggard than you remember, with droopy pockets under his eyes. He's quite a bit older than you are. He asks if he looks thinner, and you say maybe a little, and he says he hasn't been eating, it's been a long story these past few months. But he likes himself this way.

"I don't know," you try teasing him. "I have a rule that I never sleep with anyone who weighs less than me."

He looks at you doubtfully and then draws himself up to seem bigger and taller. *"Va bene?"* he asks.

"Well, maybe."

"The only rule you should have, *signorina,* is never to sleep with a man who likes his body better than yours." He takes your hand. *"Andiamo."*

You walk across the wide piazza, glancing at each other with shy surprise and frank expectation. You ask him where you're going and he senses that you feel uncomfortable going directly to the hotel, so he suggests stopping to have a coffee. You go to order, and he admires the clean brass bar with its worn patina; it's so great to be in Italy, he says, the only really authentic old bars are in Italy. He gets his espresso and your cappuccino and you lean against the bar and talk about the flight, about the Milanese guy who gave you a ride and why you were late, you talk about nothing, and finally he says you must be tired. He mentions that he has found a charming little hotel nearby. In

Milano, filled with big, anonymous modern business hotels, that is a kind of miracle.

You walk up a crooked side street in the old section of town to an ancient building with a huge door. You climb wide stone stairs to land at a cheerful airy hotel, with hand-painted furniture, fresh flowers, and views of the historic center. Inside the room, everything suddenly seems so small, so intimate. He puts down your suitcase and you don't know what to do.

"A shower?" he asks, and you nod, good idea, and disappear into the bathroom. You spend a long time in there, staring into the mirror and wondering what you're doing here with this man in Milano, and then you return, refreshed, with some courage, and flop down on the bed next to him, tossing away your towel. Ah, he says, running his finger down your spine. He caresses you and your weariness from the long flight turns into dreaminess as you make love. His warm body and his light touch, his faint smell of cigars, seem familiar and comforting. Afterward, he strokes your hair and whispers that he is going out for a couple of hours, so you should nap after that long flight, but not too much.

In what seems like a moment he is back again, and he opens the curtains so you can watch the fading light outside. He climbs back under the fluffy comforter and you think, you have only two days and nights together, maybe you will never get out of bed.

But eventually you dress and stroll outside to the nearby castle grounds. He asks you how your divorce is going and you say, you feel better, it's been a year now since he left, and you just want to cut the ties completely and get on with your life.

"And so have you had any new lovers by now?" he asks, playful, enjoying the illicitly, explicitly sexual nature of your relationship.

"Not really. San Francisco is a desert for dates."

"Don't worry," he says. "It's early."

"Maybe, but the shock of being single after so many years is the feeling that women over thirty-five are no longer considered attractive, not even by men over thirty-five."

He sighs, leading you from the castle grounds to the park nearby. "It's a shame. American men must be superficial. They want youth and beauty right up front in their faces. That isn't interesting. European men like to *discover* what's beautiful about a woman. Every woman is a mystery, and you have to find what makes her most beautiful and gives her the most pleasure."

You smile, even though you know he never seems to find women his own age all that mysterious, either. He considers women in their late thirties and early forties attractive, all right, but he is fast approaching fifty.

"Your beauty for instance," he explains, "sneaks up on you." It isn't obvious; he didn't see it right at first, he says, meeting you over breakfast in a *pensione* on an island, reading your guidebook, asking practical questions, so serious. He had to figure out how to make you smile that soft smile, which wasn't easy. "That's the pleasure."

"Were you thinking about sleeping with me when you met me?" you ask.

"Could be," he says.

"And what if I had been a silly German girl, like you thought?"

"I wouldn't have ruled it out." He takes your arm.

You aren't so sure what to think about that. "And so, when you met me, did you think I would want to sleep with you?"

"My dear, you ask too many questions." He raises an eyebrow. "When a woman tells you she has a plan to leave that morning, and then changes her mind to climb a mountain with you, you have to figure it's about eighty percent certain."

"You're terrible!" you say playfully.

"Yes, of course," he says in English. "I am terrible." And then in Italian, "But not as terrible as you."

You love remembering the excitement of that first uncertain day together.

Now he can't resist asking you. "When you saw me at breakfast, did you want to make love to me?"

"Not necessarily," you say. "Women don't decide that so quickly."

"You see, I know you better than you know yourself."

You walk quietly for a while on the parkway paths, watching teenagers milling about, clustered around tape players, talking loudly, smoking cigarettes. He squeezes your hand and you ask about his long winter.

"It was difficult," he explains. His wife had fallen in love with another man and almost left him. He couldn't imagine his life away from her, from their house, their children, their routine. They'd both had little "stories" with other lovers before, that was understood, almost expected, but this was different. This threatened everything. This was a grand passion. He was scared and lonely, he says. "But exceptional circumstances make you become more exceptional." That, of course, made it a more difficult choice for his wife, he says, with empathy and no bitterness. She stayed, but now it's different, they are together but separate. It gives him more freedom to travel, though.

"Your wife," you tell him, "would have to be completely crazy to leave you." You mean it. He is grateful for that remark, and you realize that the tables are oddly turned from Ischia. He is fragile and you are stronger, comforting someone who had seemed so invulnerable. You are not the only one who has been hurt in love.

In the evening, at a busy outdoor pizza place, you talk about his new book idea, a departure from the ones he's written, and he wants your opinion; you talk about your work, his students' art projects, your families, and you realize that the conversation is much deeper than it was on Ischia, that something else is happening.

"You seem much more content than you were," he observes when the pizza arrives.

"I am better," you say, and tell him that those four days on the island helped you more than you can say.

He dismisses that. "So tell me about all your new lovers."

"There is nothing to tell."

"Dai," he says. "Come on, tell me the whole story. I like that we can talk about our secret lives together."

You sip your wine. "It's too depressing." You explain how you always seem to be attracted to smart, witty men who turn out to be narcissists. Charmed, you give them your attention, your wit, your butternut squash risotto, your trust. You give them everything. You shine their brilliance back at them, and it is all intense and exciting and *fun* until one day the lights dim a little and they see you, they see that you want something too, that you are complicated yourself, that you are real and not without your flaws. And then they stop calling.

"There is nothing wrong with being a narcissist," the professor says. *"I'm* a narcissist. It's good to love yourself."

You hope you're experiencing a language barrier. You don't like the idea of this delightful man being yet another narcissist, but it crosses your mind as a distinct possibility.

"It's not good to love yourself to the exclusion of others, as a way to hide a deep insecurity," you say.

"That's an egoist," he says. "That's another story. Let's hear about the American egoists."

You tell him about how you flirted with a smart, charming, witty architect you had vaguely known for years at a party, danced with him, had a romantic dinner with him, and then he invited you up to his ski house for a few days.

"Ah," says the professor, interested. This looked promising.

You had a sparky conversation on the way up to the mountains, made dinner together with a nice bottle of wine, and then the architect built a fire, spread a blanket in front of it, lit a candle, and offered you a back rub.

"Back rub?" asks M., "what is 'back rub'?"

"Massage," you explain. "American foreplay."

"Not bad," he says. He takes a bite of his pizza and comments on the good anchovies.

So, you continue, the guy gave you a massage, and right at the moment when he might have kissed you, he started telling you about the woman he was in love with. The woman was just his type, he said, dark-haired, quiet, and slim with angular features—the very opposite of you, as it happens. He talked on and on about their tortured relationship—her always pushing him away but never completely letting him go, his fascination with her—while you sat up and pulled the blanket around you, listening, stupefied at how you'd misread the situation, realizing that he was completely oblivious to how you might have been interpreting the whole cabin-in-the-woods scenario. He finished his story and stared into the fire, in his own private funk. Then all at once he seemed to remember you were there, and abruptly showed you to your room, telling you, like an older brother, to sleep tight.

"Incredibile," says M., putting down his knife. He was almost angry. "This would never happen with a Frenchman. Never."

"It was my fault," you say. "I was making up a fantasy because I just wanted to be with someone. But it did nothing for my ego, that he was so uninterested in me that it never even crossed his mind that the situation was, at the very least, ambiguous."

"He is a buffoon," says the professor. "He wanted to flirt for his ego, after what happened with the other woman." He picks up his knife again and cuts a corner of his pizza. "In France, you would never tell a woman you were with, giving a massage, about being more attracted to another woman. That is outrageous."

You tell him more tales from your forays into the San Francisco singles scene. There was the plastic surgeon. You should have known better than to get involved with a plastic surgeon—he introduced himself as an ear, nose and throat doctor—but you were trying to keep an open mind. He too was smart and charming, and there was something playful about him. But over dinner one evening, he told you in graphic detail how he would redo your nose to make you more attractive. You'd never felt bad about your nose before, which is a little pug—it gets sunburned between the nostrils—but now you feel self-conscious about it. The surgeon said he could just shave a little cartilage off the sides, and then put an implant on the tip . . .

"Stop!" says the professor, gesturing at his plate. "We're eating." He sips his wine. "Forget the surgeon. Who else?"

You think about the other men you dated, the ones you

waited anxiously to hear back from, kicking yourself for coming across as too awkward and eager at first, doing everything on a date except what all your friends advised, which was to just relax and be yourself. But being yourself doesn't include going out on blind dates, period. "I have post-traumatic stress disorder with men," you say. The professor looks confused, so you explain. "If a man shows the slightest bit of interest in me, I take it as a threat that he can hurt me as much as my husband did, and I overreact accordingly. Then, of course, they lose interest."

He smiles. "Listen to you, all that psychology. It's no wonder you attract men who are complicated," he says.

"I can't help it," you say.

"And what about me? I am not complicated."

"You're different. There's no risk with you. As my psychologist says, you are *una fantasma.*"

"Una fantasma?" he asks, looking completely baffled. "I've never thought about being a *fantasma* before."

You don't understand his confusion, and just sit there eating your pizza until it dawns on you what you had said. "I didn't mean to call you a ghost," you say. "I meant a fantasy, *una fantasia.*"

"That's better. I can live with being a fantasy." He looks pleased, considering it. "But you talk about me with your psychologist?"

"Sure," you say.

"And he gives you advice?"

You nod. *"She."*

"You Americans with your psychologists! Talking about lovers like you were at a tea party." He catches the waiter's attention, making a little sipping gesture to order coffee.

"It's just for a little while. It helped when my husband left me.

Otherwise, I would have blamed myself for the whole thing. Now I just blame myself for getting involved with the wrong kind of a guy."

He grunts. "Okay, but now you don't need a psychologist any more, *cara*. Save your money, and spend it on traveling and good food." He drinks his espresso and then looks at you with his weary blue eyes. "It's simple. You're a baby. All you need is an older man who can handle you, who will take care of you, who will love to have sex with you." He waved his hand, dismissing it all. "You need someone like me in San Francisco."

"Perhaps," you say. "But maybe not married." And hopefully, you think to yourself, just a little less vain.

He shrugs. "Maybe not."

After dinner, you walk over to the Piazza del Duomo and have a grappa in an open-air bar. A wind comes up and it starts to pour. You abandon your drinks, splash through the streets, and take refuge in the covered market square, which is empty. You watch him leaning against a stone pillar and tell him he looks good from a distance, very sexy. He tells you that you should drink grappa more often. He walks closer and wipes your face dry with his foulard. Alone in the market square, with lettuce leaves scattered at your feet, you make out like teenagers, rain splattering all around.

The next morning you wake up, curled against the man next to you, and think you're with your husband. You slowly realize where you are, and sink back into your pillow. You're with the professor in Italy, as if in a dream.

You wonder what you'll do that day in gray Milano, not really caring. The professor wakes up and rings right away to have pots of café au lait brought to the room. Then you sit up in bed, naked, with a breakfast tray in front of you, enjoying the illicit crumbs on the covers, and ask him what the plan is for the day. What is there to see in Milano, has he been to the museums? The professor drinks his coffee and when he is sufficiently awake, he says that since you're island specialists, you'll have to go to an island. He puts on his green jeans and tapestry vest, slips some cigarettes into his jacket pocket, and wraps his Egyptian scarf around his neck, ready for the day. You dress and follow him to the train, with no idea where it will take you, just watching the scenery change from the city into ugly industrial outskirts and finally open country.

An hour later you arrive in Stresa, a lovely little town on the edge of a lake, Lago Maggiore. You walk down the steep streets to the wide boardwalk lined with Liberty-style villas and flowers everywhere—azaleas, rhondodendra, roses. The professor points to a villa behind a high stone wall, in a shambles.

"Can you imagine that the villas are abandoned in this beautiful place?" he asks. "I would be happy living here." You walk to the edge of the enormous lake, surrounded by high granite mountains and green valleys, and take a water taxi to Isola Bella, "beautiful island."

The island at first seems to be covered with bad restaurants and tourist kiosks selling the same Botticelli Venus-on-the-ashtrays that they sell everywhere in Italy. But then you enter the Palazzo Borromeo, Conte Vitaliano Borromeo's 1670 hideaway, and suddenly, you are in another world. The huge palace rests on the edge of the island cliffs, and you walk through room after room of overdone gilded splendor. Here is a grand ballroom, there is the canopied bed where Napoleon slept (twice, behind Josephine's back: once with an Italian princess, another with an opera star), there is a little stage with fierce marionettes that must have terrorized the children. The professor explains that the way you can tell this is a Baroque, instead of Renaissance, room is that you have the feeling that you can't escape, you don't see the other rooms or have a sense of the building as a whole. It is handy, you think, to have an affair with an art professor.

You pass by rooms filled with armor and wind down spiral stone stairs into the grottoes. "Incredible," says the professor, and you have never seen anything like it, either. The cool cellars are lined, floor to ceiling, in mosaics made of pebbles, in sea themes, with swirling shells, starfish, and mermaids, room after room of fantastic designs. There is a smooth white marble sculpture of a woman sleeping on her stomach, with a pretty curve in her back. "That," says the professor, "is obscenely beautiful."

The grottoes open out into classic Italian gardens, with infinite varieties of exotic trees, plants, and flowers. Huge terracotta pots of lemon trees and geraniums perch atop the cliffs against deep blue water shimmering in the background. White peacocks traipse around the lawns, displaying their spectacular tails whenever a drab little peahen shows the slightest interest. Delicate, pastel-colored water lilies float in a reflecting pool. Statues of gods and mythical beasts face the lake, fending off invaders, standing at attention on ever-higher terraces of roses. You explore the gardens together, taking twisting paths, and are comfortable not saying anything at all.

The sun breaks out and the professor sits down in an ornate iron chair on a lawn. "Imagine it in the evening, at a party, lit everywhere with candles, with a banquet there and a string orchestra over there," he says, gesturing. "You and I were born several centuries too late." You picture him telling tales in *The*

Decameron, sneaking off between story-telling sessions into the grottoes or a secluded corner of the gardens.

Reluctantly, you leave the palace grounds and your fantasy life and stand in line for a boat to another island. You hear someone call your name. You turn and see a woman who seems familiar but whom you can't quite place. Then you realize she's a foreign student who lived with you six years before; you've bumped into absolutely the only person you know in Switzerland right here near the border. You are so surprised that when you try to introduce the woman to the professor you completely forget his name. You chat for a while but then it comes back to you that you never really liked the Swiss woman, and even if it is a phenomenal coincidence to see her, you hope she sits somewhere else on the boat, because you only have one day with the professor, and you don't want to spend any of it with her. The Swiss woman's boyfriend calls her to come take her seat, and so she leaves in a flurry of air kisses. The professor watches all of this and you tell him it was remarkable to run into her, but in fact you weren't ever really friends.

"I noticed that right away," he says. "Now I know something new about you: you can be cold." You say you hope you hadn't been rude.

"No, no," he says. "It's just nice to know you're so warm to me when you can be so chilly to others. It makes it that much better."

You stroll around another island—Isola Madre—taking trails that snake through lush woods to wide flowery meadows thick with exotic birds. He watches some parrots, and tells you a story about a time a little Italian girl ran up to him screaming, pointing at his face, saying he had a *pappagallo* nose. He has a good sense of humor about himself, especially since he really does have a parrot nose.

The professor pulls out a cigar, finds a bench, and starts smoking. You sit there quietly for a long time, looking at the gardens, the birds, and the ocean beyond. "We've seen so many lovely things today," he finally says, content.

"Amazing," you say. It had been as enchanting as a day on Ischia, but completely different.

Snuggling on the train ride home, he touches your arm tenderly, easily. You think about the habit of the American men you've encountered who jump right into sexual intimacy, but then worry that if they touch you outside of sex you'll want to marry them. They confuse a woman's desire for affection with demands on their freedom. It's nice to be touched with an easy familiarity that says nothing about possession or expectations.

It's late and you're hungry when you return to the hotel, but hungrier for each other. He caresses your ass and tells you, *mi piace tutto il tuo corpo,* I like your body, I like all of it. He pulls one edge of your underwear tight, and then releases it. You are so sensual, he says. You play and play and he keeps offering more, licking you and lightly pinching your breasts, until you are out of your head with pleasure, you can't tell where one orgasm stops and another one begins, riding bigger and bigger waves, the surf crashing over you, spinning you underwater, and when you finally drift back to shore and can speak again you tell him, loosely translating a French phrase he has used, that he has killed you so many times you are dead.

Famished, you go outside and wander in the old Jewish section of town, deciding against several bright restaurants, until you find a dark trattoria tucked in a side street. You always have great luck together finding good places to eat. You both order risotto milanese, with its rich aroma and saffron flavor, and you suspect that the reason it tastes so good has to do with veal broth, and even though you are a vegetarian, you don't care. It crosses your mind that maybe you shouldn't be a vegetarian at all anymore. He orders veal with porcini mushrooms, and you taste one, placing the dark, earthy mushroom in your mouth. As it melts you look across the table and wonder whether you'll ever have a chance to have another meal like this, with the professor, again.

It makes you sad, to have to leave so soon. He has to catch a train early in the morning, and then you would be off to visit friends in Bologna, Verona, and Florence. This visit will become another snapshot of paradise that you will tuck away in your desk.

He seems to sense what you are thinking. "What are you doing in September?"

You've forgotten all about September, and a nervous thrill shivers through you, but you calmly say you have no real plans.

"I've never been to California," he says. "I think I would like San Francisco."

You don't say anything. You try to digest that while you walk back to the hotel. You're excited and scared. You can't imagine what you would do with M. in your world.

"Maybe you should come visit sometime," you finally say.

"An invitation!" M. exclaims. He will probably be free in September. He says nothing more about it.

In the morning, you have early trains. This time when he kisses you good-bye in the train station, it isn't so bittersweet. It seems like you might see each other again, but it seems just as likely that you are pretending.

FIVE

SAN FRANCISCO

It is a long, gray summer. Whenever you drive outside the thick curtain of fog that circles your immediate world, you are surprised to see that the sun is blazing hot. It makes you wonder why you live here in the middle of February when it is August everywhere else, why you pay the price you pay to be a San Franciscan.

You moved to San Francisco after college on a whim, because it seemed to be a city full of people with whims. You were lured by the city's improbable terrain, its Old-Worldish charm, and its history of bemused tolerance for all kinds of misfits. You thought San Francisco would be a place where you could settle and still have the sense of traveling, of wandering well-known streets and always being surprised. So you drove someone else's big Buick Riviera all the way west, and when you finally crossed the Golden Gate Bridge, taking the scenic route in, you had a gleeful feeling that you had found what you were looking for. You were home.

Even though there are some 750,000 people living in this

seven-by-seven-mile city, San Francisco has the feeling of what the Italians call *una città a dimensione d'uomo*. It is a human-sized city, where you can walk to buy your bread in one shop and your produce in another, where you can cover the distance from Bay to beach in an afternoon on foot. There has always been room in San Francisco, as in a small town, for oddball characters, who are as cheerfully accepted as the absurdly steep hills the houses are built on. It has always been possible here to make do on the margins, to experiment and dream, to find others who believe that they, too, can live off their writing, their art, their politics; that they can follow their passions and never mind the price of real estate. Or at least it always used to be like that.

Lately, though, you've begun to feel as if your love affair with the city has turned into a bad marriage. You live in the Haight-Ashbury, where you used to be able to share huge, high-ceilinged apartments for relatively little money, but now the hippies left over from the Summer of Love are homeless, on a permanently bad trip, and everyone else is worried about getting evicted. You watch as the character of the city changes, as baby-faced Internet entrepreneurs and Lexus lawyers push the artists, dreamers, and immigrants into tighter and tighter corners. Suddenly the dot-com people have come to town, in droves. They move here not because it is San Francisco but because it is a quaint place to live and be only an hour away from Silicon Valley. Housing prices have taken quantum leaps, and it has become impossible for people like the person you were fifteen years ago to move to San Francisco, not without stock options or a trust fund.

Divorced, with little connection to the net economy, you find the city that has always sparkled for you has now become dull. The romance has left San Francisco the way you feel the youth and attractiveness have drained out of your face. Now, you feel invisible on the sidewalks. You've stopped being able to meet people the way you used to. You aren't so old, but everyone seems younger, wealthier, more attractive, with so many more people to call on their cell phones. You've always felt lucky that you got San Francisco in the divorce—your husband moved to the suburbs to live with his girlfriend—but some days it doesn't seem like such a prize. Sometimes, especially when it is coldly clammy out in the summer, you think it might be better to just leave, to find a new home.

Then one day a postcard of a silver propeller plane lands in your mail from the French professor. You've thought about him from time to time, lingering over his postcards, but have mostly banished him from your mind. He is a fantasy, and you have to be realistic, pull your life together. It's been a couple of months since you've heard from him, and you assumed he must have found another vacation friend. He had mentioned that he'd like to visit San Francisco in September, but you were sure it wouldn't happen.

Now he writes in English that he is "very exciting to come," and he's made a flight reservation for San Francisco, staying for twelve days. During that time, he says, he will be entirely under your responsibility. He is leaving everything about your amorous trip for you to decide, since you know his tastes: charming hotels, big, comfy beds, and out-of-the-way surprises.

You drop the card. It's impossible. How can you spend almost two weeks on your own turf with a man you've known for only a few days, in a fantasy world of islands and antique hotels? You won't be able to sustain the romance. He will become bored with you and your mundane little world. He will sneer at your shabby flat and think the art is bad and that you have way too many pairs of shoes hidden under the bed. He'll be appalled at how often you check your phone messages and e-mail. After believing for a few short days in Italy that you are an amusing, well-read woman of the world, he will see through all that and leave thinking that you are just another ugly American. And you will never see him again.

You ignore the postcard for a few days. Then you catch yourself, making your usual rounds of the city, thinking how surprised he would be at the steep hills, how charmed by the rows of Victorian houses, how he probably has never seen anything like a redwood tree. You find a postcard of a couple driving a 1950s convertible on the beach and write that he is indeed "very exciting to come," and finally drop it, dog-eared, in a mailbox. He sends back a photo of the Golden Gate Bridge disappearing into the fog and you realize that he *really* has his sights set on San Francisco. He has spent only three days in the United States in his life, in New York City fifteen years ago, and now you are responsible for his once-in-a-lifetime trip to California.

Well, you say to yourself, pulling out some maps, he's a lucky guy. You study the maps and come up with a plan for twelve perfect days in California, your California, and you send him a postcard promising him an island, too.

The day finally comes when the professor is supposed to arrive. You spend the whole morning taking down all the art in the flat, rearranging it, wondering if he will think those family photos too sentimental, that watercolor not well done, and then you put them all back where they were in the first place. You change your clothes several times, too, trying on various outfits that all seem to make you look unsophisticated. Eventually you give up and put on your favorite worn jeans and cowboy boots because you figure he might as well know right off the bat that you aren't even trying to impersonate a European intellectual or a delicate French beauty. You are a big, healthy American blonde.

You wait in the international terminal as homebound passengers roll their trolleys toward open-armed relatives and weary honeymooners catch their first glimpse of this notoriously romantic city. Finally you see the familiar denim jacket, Egyptian scarf, silver bracelet and chestnut curls. The professor embraces you and you absolutely can't believe you are there at San Francisco International Airport, picking up a man you met over breakfast on an Italian island a year ago, a man in whose company you've spent a total of six days.

"Hi," you say in English, and at first you can't remember a word of Italian, nothing comes out at all. You smile shyly and lead him out of the maze to the parking lot elevators in silence, hoping that you will even be able to communicate with each other for twelve days.

"Thirteen hours," he says, when you finally reach the outdoor parking lot. "Can I smoke yet?"

"Sorry," you tell him. "California is a nonsmoking state." He has a moment of panic before he sees you are joking, and you both relax a little as he lights up.

You toss his battered leather bag into the car, afraid to glance at him, concentrate on driving, and head for home on the industrial freeway, passing big Internet billboards and bald brown hills. He is puzzled by the ugliness and you remind him, your Italian coming back, that the highway to the airport is ugly in Paris, too. You exit and turn onto hilly Dolores Street, a stately boulevard of palm trees and Victorian houses, and he begins to become excited. You wind up a very steep back hill toward the Haight-Ashbury, holding the car with the hand brake at a stop sign to keep it from rolling backward, and as he grabs on to the corners of his seat the entire city comes into view, from the hills of houses to the toy blocks and triangles downtown. He is entranced. Over and over he says, *"Non ci posso credere."* I can't believe I'm here.

You park a few blocks from your flat and warn him that your place is bohemian. He is delighted by the worn Victorians on the street, surprised at the long line of homeless people waiting for lunch at a church nearby, and intensely interested in everything you are used to seeing every day and never notice. You open the gate to the 1907 apartment building where you live and lead him upstairs. He surveys the high ceilings, hardwood floors, molded wainscoting, cheerful kitchen, haphazard furniture, and books everywhere and pronounces the whole place charming. He notices the laundry strung on a line from your living room window out to a tree in the garden and comments, *"Il sistema napoletano."* While you explain about not having a clothes dryer, he walks right into your room and hops onto the bed.

"Monumentale," he says, patting the mattress. While you tell him how it had been kind of important and symbolic to get a really good bed after your divorce, how you had tried them all out like the princess and the pea, he starts to kiss and caress you. It is surprising how, after a moment's hesitation, when you feel like a total stranger, miles away, the intimacy returns and you're comfortable together again, just reaching over and touching each other.

He is too wide awake to lie around napping, so you take him for a quick tour. You walk down grimy Haight Street, with its tattoo parlors, pseudo-Summer-of-Love head shops, used clothing stores, burrito restaurants, and teenybopper boutiques, and the professor stops in front of almost every window, fascinated. You are tired of the Haight after all these years, but today it seems like a friendly street carnival. You recount stories about the sixties rock stars who used to live in the neighborhood—the Grateful Dead around the corner from your house, Jimi Hendrix in that red house, maybe Janis Joplin in your own building, but then everyone says that about his or her building. You tell him how there used to be old sofas in the revival movie house, and how much you like it that after so many years you know the people in the produce market, the independent bookstore, the post office, and the hardware store. For all its fake-sixties tourist appeal, for all its gentrification (the worst building in the neighborhood is worth a million bucks), for all the mom-and-pop businesses that have been forced to move away, it is still a real neighborhood. A scraggly guy in a beard and Mexican vest near the park offers you buds and doses, *sotto voce,* and when you translate what he said, the professor relishes the fact that there he is on the famous hippie Haight Street, and someone is actually trying to sell him drugs.

You cross over into Golden Gate Park, half as long as the city itself, a variegated jewel that never would have been built if it were up to anyone today. You stroll through the tunnel near the entrance of the park, where someone ingeniously molded stalactites onto the ceiling years ago, and then emerge into the sun. On a nearby hill, drummers are drumming African drums, barefoot women in Indian skirts are dancing, guys in long baggy shorts are throwing Frisbees, and people are lying out barechested, catching the last rays before the chill.

"This is just how I imagined San Francisco," says the professor, and it was how you imagined it, too, before you moved here. You walk over to the Hall of Flowers, closed since it was battered by a big storm a few years earlier, and the professor gasps at the beauty of the fragile glass palace surrounded by palm trees and tidy beds of flowers. You show him the huge square of dahlias nearby, bursting in color, and point out the rocks that someone has arranged into a miniature model of the Grand Canyon. He can't believe the park is so vast and uncrowded, and you've hardly seen any of it yet. It has been so long since you've actually looked around the park instead of bicycling through, unseeing, just getting exercise.

The sun sets and you walk back toward home, veering off to Cole Valley, which is near the Haight but in another, tidier, more upscale world. The professor admires how European the neighborhood is, with its cheese shop, its sleek blond-wood restaurants, its compact bars and cafés. He is hungry, so you duck into your favorite sushi restaurant on a side street, a plain place with plastic chairs, decorated with old Japanese calendars. You order the sushi adventurously, happy to be taking a Parisian to a meal he could never get in Paris without paying a small fortune. He savors every bite of fish and marvels at its freshness. The sushi chef comes over to the table to tell you that you have such good taste that next time you're in he promises he'll feed you a really exquisite fish liver. It's perfect: of all the many times you've been in this little restaurant, the chef waits until you're there with a snobbish Parisian to compliment you on your palate. You walk the few short blocks home, where the professor says he already feels comfortable. He lights a cigar even though no one ever smokes in your house, and watches the church lights glow in the distance.

In the morning you're surprised to wake up and find someone in your bed. You open the curtains on the bay windows for a view of the big, secret backyards in the neighborhood, and bring him coffee as he wakes up. He sips tentatively, his first American coffee, and is surprised that it is so good. Of course it's good, you tell him. You're in San Francisco.

That day you take him along for the ride, showing him the collective writers' office where you work.

You're anxious about introducing the professor to the people you work with, even though they like him already from your stories about him. They've heard about your divorce and all your dating disasters over the past year and a half, and they've heard about the professor and know he's the one man in all that time who has made you feel happy.

But it's odd to have your fantasy world meet your reality. You worry about what people will think about this dalliance with a married Frenchman. Some of your other friends have been surprised and disapproving. One told you that maybe it wasn't so healthy, being involved with someone who was safe because he was unavailable; maybe it was getting in the way of your being able to meet someone appropriate. Another asked you how you were any different from the woman your husband had escaped your marriage with, the woman he was seeing on the side who knew darn well that he was recently married and that she was interfering with the possibility that you could resolve things by yourselves.

But you know there is a world of difference, that you are no threat to the professor and his wife, that they are French people who have a clear understanding that the professor isn't going to leave his wife and move in with an American woman next week.

You have lunch at a Thai restaurant with two of the women

you work with, and even though they don't speak much of the same languages—a bit of French, some English and Italian—the professor begins to believe that all the women in San Francisco are smart, well-traveled, and like to laugh. Your friends pronounce him charming and sexy, which he loves hearing repeated.

Afterward, you drive to Mount Tamalpais, the big sleeping woman that looms over Marin County. You park at the trailhead to the secret entrance to Muir Woods, where you can descend into the tall trees hardly ever seeing a tourist. You do pass one, a Danish man at a vista point, who complains to you that there is nothing to see. You shrug and translate that to the professor, who opens his arms wide to the fog rolling in from the sea, licking the flanks of the hills. "There is everything," he says.

You walk in silence on the dark trail, taking in the prehistoric ferns and soft needles under your feet. Finally you tell the professor what has bothered you since he arrived, that you are worried that after twelve days he'll get tired of you.

"Maybe," he says, "but after twelve days you might get tired of me, too." He takes your hand and tells you that you are a sweet woman, you are easy to be with. You tell him he is welcome to his space whenever he needs it, trying to say that in Italian. He nods soberly, agreeing, and then tries to suppress a laugh. You don't understand what is so funny and he explains that he can't help it, it's just too much, a Californian talking like that about having space. You tell him to "visualize" himself abandoned on a California trail and he grabs on tightly to your arm.

You keep descending toward the creek until you are level with the tops of the redwoods, rooted far below. You climb down the trail through the trees and light bursts in between great soft branches, dappling the forest floor. You take a path that ends up winding around huge tree stumps and cathedral circles of redwoods. *"Impressionante,"* says the professor, staring up. "There is nothing like this in Europe." You hike back to the top of the trail, check into a cozy mountain inn there, and have a drink on the terrace, watching San Francisco peek between the distant hills like the Emerald City.

"Wonderful," says the professor, putting his feet up on the redwood railing on the deck. "Gorgeous."

You remember being on another terrace with him, overlooking the Mediterranean, and feel the same sense of luxuriating in a perfect moment.

The next morning you drive down the curving road to Stinson Beach. It is the first time the professor has seen the Pacific Ocean. "It may be called pacific," he says, "but it doesn't seem peaceful at all compared with the Mediterranean. And so cold!"

You walk barefoot in the sand until you find a cluster of rocks that you could climb on to stretch out in the morning sun, watching the waves crash. He searches around to see if there is anyone watching, if you could get away with making love on the beach. The idea tickles you and then you flash on a time Jon wanted to make love on that same beach, so full of desire, so dead now, and you wonder whether you will ever feel free and sexy at home without feeling haunted.

Eventually you make your way back to San Francisco along the rugged coast, a coastline that reminds him of Spain. You drive over the Golden Gate Bridge, its orange girders bright against the blue sky, and on this miraculously clear morning you can see from Mount Diablo in the east, to the sailboats beneath you on the bay, to the tidy vertical stripes of streets along the flanks of San Francisco, all the way to the Farallon Islands out in the ocean. You make your way across and into the Marina District, where you visit the Palace of Fine Arts, a Roman-style rotunda built in 1915 for the Panama-Pacific International Exposition, which you love because it is encircled by huge statues of terra-cotta women who are facing butt-out to the world, making fun of the whole business of imposing city monuments.

You head across the city and do what you've never done before—you drive down Lombard Street, the crookedest street in the world. When the professor is surprised at the extreme zigzags, you act like it is just another normal street in San Francisco, and you drive into North Beach, San Francisco's Italian section.

"It's unreal." He sighs with delight, taking it all in. "A doll's city."

The professor announces, with his new California vocabulary, that he wants to "take his space," and is going to explore the city by himself for a while. It makes you nervous to abandon him, but you realize that he has traveled the world by himself and will be able to figure out how to get to the Museum of Modern Art by four o'clock. So you go back to your office.

When you see him again, meeting up at the museum, he has the city all figured out. He has discovered Chinatown, says the financial district has no charm, and that the shop windows are boring to look at. He strides through the art museum, making his snap art professor judgments: the early Calder works are interesting, you rarely see those, that Matisse is beautiful, Clyfford Still is no big deal, and he isn't so sure about California hyper-realism. He pauses at a glass cube and explains that he can lecture for three hours about that glass cube. You ask what he could possibly say and he becomes animated.

"This chair!" he exclaims, pointing to a clean, simple metal-

and-leather seat in the middle of the room. "This chair would not have been possible without this cube." He points to a woman in black. "Calvin Klein would not have been possible without this cube, without minimalism." He talks about the object just being what it is, what you see, positive and negative spaces. You are amused by his performance, his almost boyish enthusiasm for holding forth on art.

You take him home for dinner, and do what you have missed most since you were married—you tantalize all his senses with a meal: fresh mozzarella and summer tomatoes with basil and olive oil; good crusty sourdough bread; orecchiette pasta with cauliflower, anchovies, toasted pine nuts, currants soaked in white wine, and a sprinkling of parmigiano-reggiano cheese; salad greens with olive oil, shallots, and lemon. He abandons himself to the meal and the wine and can't help himself, he has another serving. You bring him espresso and an alembic brandy made in Ukiah that you say is better than most French cognac, and he agrees. He smokes a cigar and you smoke one of the Gitanes cigarettes he sent you last year for Christmas and then, completely satisfied, you make yourselves dessert.

For the next two days, you pretend to be out of town and play San Francisco tourists. You have an errand to do on tony upper Fillmore Street, and the professor is pleased to see that there is a smart section of town, full of little shops with clever window dressing. He is less bohemian than he lets on. You take him to Fisherman's Wharf to catch a ferry, and are amused to see the professor of the philosophy of aesthetics pawing through a bin in a souvenir shop looking for T-shirts to bring home to his kids.

You climb up to a friend's apartment on the Filbert Steps, a steep garden staircase with quirky wooden houses perched on the sides, where you have a drink and watch the sky turn pink with the Bay Bridge in the background. Suddenly a flock of bright green parrots flies into view, just another little daily San Francisco miracle. You hurry to climb to the top of Coit Tower while it's still light, and you realize that never in fifteen years have you been up there to see the sunset. You tell him the story of Lillie Coit, who built the three-story fire tower as a monument to her fondness for firemen. It is a glorious, rare day, and you take in all the territory from the hills of North Beach to Mount Tamalpais and Tiburon. Even after all these years, you can't believe all of this is in your backyard.

You hike down to a trendy bar in North Beach to watch people, checking out whether the couples fit together, deciding if you like their clothes, making catty comments about them all in Italian. Then you cross the street to eat at one of your favorite restaurants, a tiny, unpretentious *osteria* where the food tastes like Tuscany and there are few tourists. You steer him to City Lights bookstore, talking about the Beats, and you have a late drink at Vesuvio's bar, a charming place papered with poetry and original art, with a Victorian chandelier that was lit with candles after the most recent earthquake. You are visiting all the places you used to love to wander with Jon on a Sunday afternoon, reclaiming territory you've avoided, happy the romance of North Beach has outlived your marriage.

The next morning, you take M. to the Castro, the city's gay district, rainbow flag fluttering at the portal. He is fascinated by the men casually walking around in couples. The Castro, you tell him, isn't as lively as it was in the early eighties, before AIDS made it a kind of living ghost town. But it is becoming brighter again. You show him the magnificent gilded Castro Theatre, where the Mighty Wurlitzer rises before shows and the organist plays theme music to match the film, always ending with "San Francisco, Open Your Golden Gate" as it descends, the entire audience singing and clapping and whooping it up.

When you stop for a mid-morning coffee, the professor asks you how to order. "An espresso, please," you tell him, and he practices. He orders his coffee, and then you order yours. The professor overhears.

"What did you ask for?" he says.

"Coffee," you say.

"No," he says, "you said something else."

"Half-decaf, low-fat, medium extra-hot latte, no foam," you say.

"You're kidding me. So complicated! You're torturing these people working at the coffee bar. Why don't you just order coffee?"

You shrug. "It's normal here."

That afternoon, you have a few of your friends over to meet the professor. Drinking wine in your wild garden—one of your friends kindly says that it looks much tidier in the summer, which isn't exactly true—the professor is impressed by how Americans are not at all like what he had expected. He compliments one of your friends, a journalist in his sixties, for speaking French perfectly, with no trace of an accent. He says that your Italian-speaking graphic designer friend, a fine-boned fifty-year-old with a strong sense of style, is the type of woman who would be at home in any great city in the world. He is only a little confused by an artist friend who wears vintage housedresses; you have to explain that she isn't really like a midwestern woman from the 1950s, that she wears those clothes a bit ironically.

You are surprised, there in the garden, to find yourself happy—with your friends, your home, with the professor. If he lived in San Francisco, if there were any possibility that he could break your heart, you never would allow yourself the pleasure of him for fear of the pain. You know he'll be leaving in a week, but that still seems far enough away not to anticipate the sadness. For that one moment, you are completely content. The professor has not only opened your heart a crack, he has made you open your eyes and fall back in love with your city, your life, your friends.

When the light dims, your young Italian-speaking friend Elena leaves, tossing you a set of keys. The professor asks what those are for, and you tell him, the convertible. You can't go to southern California without a convertible, can you?

{SIX}

LOS ANGELES

The next morning, you pull the convertible around to the front of the building, where the professor is waiting, bag in hand.

"Wanna ride?" you say in English.

He breaks into a smile, taking in the big gold American convertible with its white leather interior, very Los Angeles.

You load everything into the car, the professor checking out all the controls, as delighted as a child. "I never imagined I'd be driving in California in a *macchina decapitata* with a blonde," he says. "This is too perfect." A "decapitated car," it turns out, is not the best translation for "convertible," but it works. You're learning the professor's version of Italian, which isn't exactly infallible, and by mixing in a little French and English, you're starting to develop a language of your own.

"Road trip," you say, sliding a Van Morrison CD into the player.

"Where are we going?" he asks.

"Los Angeles," you say, "plus a surprise." You thought you'd take the coast part of the way, past Big Sur, see some museums in L.A., go to the beach. You had, in fact, made reservations weeks before.

"But what about Yosemite?" asks the professor eagerly. "I'd like to see Yosemite. I hear it's spectacular. Let's go to Yosemite first."

You consider that. You want to make the trip perfect for the professor, but Yosemite is quite a detour from Los Angeles, the place he told you he most wanted to visit. Plus, the professor doesn't drive. He tried once, he explained, taking lessons about thirty years ago, but he said everything looked like a movie to him when he drove, and he got so caught up in the movie that he forgot he was driving. Fortunately, he's never been behind the wheel since.

"Yosemite," you say, "is far away."

"I don't know if I'll ever be back," he says, a little anxious. "How can I go to California and not see Yosemite?"

One thing you're realizing about the professor, as it dawns on you that he has a few defects, is that he is not the athletic type. He walks a lot, but only because he doesn't drive. He would consider a hike for the sake of hiking completely pointless. Yosemite with the professor would be a car experience, along with the ten thousand other cars in the valley, a little like being in the Uffizi, elbowing to see the sights.

"California," you explain, not wanting to disappoint him, "is about the size of Italy." You don't know whether that's true, but it sounds right. "We are in Milano, and we're driving to Roma. Going to Yosemite would be like taking a side trip to Venezia."

The professor thinks that over. "What about just Venezia, then?" he says. You've used the wrong comparison, because like Woody Allen, whose films he adores, the professor thinks that the only livable places in Europe are Paris and Venice, with

Barcelona a distant third. San Francisco, he's already discovered, is quaint and charming but impossibly far from the center of the world, which is, of course, Paris.

"My dear professor," you say gently, "you said you were going to leave everything up to me."

"*Va bene*," he says, letting go of Venice rather easily. He sinks back into the leather seat, puts on his sunglasses, rewraps his scarf, and checks himself out in the mirror. "A road trip," he says, repeating your phrase. "Like Humbert Humbert in *Lolita*."

"You're lucky to be with me," you say, "because Lolita wasn't old enough to drive."

"I *am* lucky to be with you, *signorina*," he says.

You drive with the top down to the outskirts of San Francisco, until you can no longer stand the chilly fog. As you leave the city heading south on a scenic route, the professor is enchanted with the hills, the open space, the live oak and wheat grass. You point out Silicon Valley in the distance, which he wants to visit. You explain that for all the fuss about Silicon Valley, there is absolutely nothing there worth seeing, no concern for the aesthetics of the real world. It's all office parks, strip malls, and highway exits. You keep heading south, past San Jose, past Gilroy, the garlic capital of the world, past farms and expanses of nothingness, music playing the whole way.

You run out of conversation somewhere around Watsonville. The professor turns to his favorite topic, sex. He wants to know the details about everyone you've dated since you saw him last.

"*Raccontami tutto,*" he says. Tell me the story about everything.

You tell him there is no story. You've lived in San Francisco long enough that you've already run into anyone you might happen to fall in love with. You've tried going to events where you might find interesting men—art openings, film festivals, parties, lectures; you even pretended to shop for a motorcycle. In the end you met a lot of really attractive, charming, gay men. You've even considered hanging around the airport to see what new single men arrive in town, but it hasn't come to that yet.

"What about the Internet?" asks the professor.

You grimace.

"It couldn't hurt to try it," says the professor, sounding a little like your mother.

"I did try it," you confess.

"Ahh." The professor brightens. "And?"

The problem with computer dating, you explain, is that it's completely superficial. People judge you right off by your age, height, weight—that sort of thing. Men who are your age or older always want women who are younger than you. And then they always say they're looking for a "slim" or "beautiful" woman. If men understood how few women would actually call themselves slim or beautiful, they'd realize why they get so few responses.

You're ranting. "One guy wanted a photo of me because he said he'd had the *really embarrassing experience* of meeting a woman for a drink who *must have weighed a hundred fifty pounds*," you say. "He said it like she was a freak or something."

"But there must be all kinds of men out there," says the professor.

"Men say they're seeking a bright, adventuresome woman with a sense of humor, and they'll spend hours trying to impress you with overly clever e-mails, but once you tell them your age or your size, they never write back. They don't really want accomplished, smart, funny women. What they really want are skinny blonde babes with big tits and big hair who will make no demands on them whatsoever—but they think it looks too crass to say so."

"Poverina," says the professor, with half-mocking sympathy. "And so you never went out with any of them."

You concentrate on driving, switching lanes, saying nothing for a while.

"I did go out with a few."

The professor turns down the CD player. "And?"

Initially, you tell him, it was great. You got a hundred responses to your ad in the first three days.

"Wow," says the professor.

"I may have exaggerated myself a little," you say, "but it did do wonders for my ego—at first." After all those months of being single, you were deleting responses left and right from interested men. Grammatical errors, right-wing politics, sport utility vehicles, "multitudinous enthusiasms," romantic walks on the beach: delete, delete, delete.

"Maybe you were too choosy?" asks the professor. You give him a look that says, What do you mean, too choosy?

"Many of them answer any ad from any breathing female, writing things like, 'I'd love to suck your pussy.' Definitely out of the question."

"Suck your pussy?" asks the professor. This was a new phrase.

"Lecca la fica," you tell him, using the Italian expression. Licking the fig. The English expression, you explain, is more like sucking a little cat.

"Vulgar," he says. "The Italian expression is much nicer."

You put a line in your ad saying, extra credit if you downhill ski, speak Italian, or know George Eliot's real name.

"One out of three isn't bad," says the professor.

"Mary Anne Evans," you say.

"Thanks," he says. "Who knows when that will come in handy."

Your first response was from Marco. Marco seemed great. He taught physics at a nearby university, played soccer, was Italian-American, liked to cook, ski, was forty years old, smart, and adorably handsome. You had a couple of glasses of wine together, and he gave you a brief kiss good night, then e-mailed you and said he'd love to see you again.

"Va bene," says the professor.

You made a date to meet each other at a bar, and he didn't show up. You were hoping he hadn't arrived early, and been put off by the fact that you had chosen a lesbian bar, and then left.

"A lesbian bar?" asks the professor. He makes an Italian gesture to indicate that you are crazy.

"It was a nice bar in my neighborhood," you explain. "I figured if he had a sense of humor about it, it would be a good sign."

"You're terrible," says the professor. Then he shifts a little toward you. "Could we go to the lesbian bar when we get back? I would *love* to go to an American lesbian bar."

You give him an evil eye and go on. The next day, you got an e-mail from Marco saying that he tried to make it to the bar, but he got pulled over by the police because they thought he was an escaped convict wanted for murder in San Diego. It could happen to anyone, you figured, so you gave him another chance.

The professor raises an eyebrow, skeptical.

When he didn't show up for a second date, you deleted him for good, but got an apologetic e-mail saying he'd had to take his cousin to the airport unexpectedly, and they ended up going to Vegas on a whim. As if there were no phones in the airport. You didn't answer, and then a month later you got another message from him saying he was really sorry, he just couldn't deal with blondes who spoke perfect Italian, they scared him.

"Your Italian," says the professor, "is hardly perfect. And you aren't even that blonde."

"Grazie mille," you say. You watch the highway signs and turn toward Monterey. Then, you go on, you had lunch with a dot-com millionaire who traveled to Italy frequently, a lot of potential, but he talked about himself the entire time, except when he was taking calls on his cell phone, an utter bore. Then you went on a bike ride with an aviation psychologist.

"Aviation psychologist?"

"The guys who figure out how many people they can cram into the back of the plane before ugly mob behavior ensues."

The professor makes a face showing great distaste.

You went on a bike ride with the guy, you say, which seemed fine until it was apparent how eager he was to beat you riding up the hill.

"And then what happened with the airplane psychologist?"

"As we rode over the Golden Gate Bridge, he asked me what I thought I had in common with Marilyn Monroe."

"Marilyn Monroe?" the professor asks, puzzled. "Why would he ask that?"

You explain that when you wrote your ad, you had tried to come up with a euphemism for slightly plump that wouldn't be negative, and wouldn't make people think you were obese, but would alert them to the fact that you aren't skinny. "Ruben-esque" was too super-sized. So you came up with "Monroesque," thinking it was a good term to indicate a little chubby but still sexy. It turned out that it had conjured up a lot of other associations, though.

"Big breasts, whispery voice, long legs, platinum hair," the professor ticks them off on his fingers.

"I know. I changed it. Instead I wrote that I am a little plump around the edges, like Kathleen Turner, halfway between *Body Heat* and *Serial Mom*."

The professor looks you over. "I don't know why you have to say anything about your body," he says. "You are too worried about it."

"Thank you," you say. So there you were in your stretchy biking shorts and helmet, trying to explain the Marilyn Monroe thing to the aviation shrink, and he gave you a look like you'd engaged in false advertising or something. After the ride, the guy—who wasn't exactly attractive himself, balding and short with no chin whatsoever, despite the unequivocal "handsome" in the ad—called you up immediately to say, "You just don't ring my chimes."

"Is that an aviation expression?" asks the professor.

"No," you say. "That is an asshole expression. There was no need for him to say anything at all. So I told him, 'That's okay,' and he said, 'I wasn't apologizing.'"

"*Maleducato*," says the professor. "I'm beginning to see what you mean about American men."

The sun comes out and you put the top down, driving over some bluffs with a view of the ocean, finally arriving at the seaside town of Carmel, where the professor has his first Mexican meal. You drive along the coast until the land widens into green grazing pastures that unroll into the calm ocean, a deceptively peaceful entrance to Big Sur. But as the road begins to wind toward bridges that hang, precariously, over wild canyons far below, the fog comes in like a wall. There is nothing to see but the narrow strip of highway a few feet in front of you, which you take all the way to Los Angeles.

You drive into L.A. with the top down, past towering palm trees, Malibu villas, swimming pools, glittering beaches—the kind of California scenery the professor says he's seen in movies and postcards but always assumed was overcolored, hyper-real.

"You have to take a photo of me in the *macchina decapitata* with a palm tree," he announces. "My friends will never believe this."

You pull off to a side road and find a suitable palm tree with the ocean in the background. You maneuver the car around until it's situated in front of the tree just so, the light making the chrome sparkle. The professor starts telling you how to take the photo.

"Shhhh," you say. "I'm the director. You're the talent." He frowns, but gives you a dashing Italian playboy look when you tell him to say "cheese." Then he insists on a photo of a California blonde in the convertible, so you fluff up your hair, stroke the interior, lean way back and give him a total surfer girl smile, very silly. You put the camera on top of the car with a timer, try to keep it from wobbling, and run around to the other side, holding on to each other to keep your balance on the edge of the road. That one turns out to be sweet.

"Okay, *signorina*," says the professor, as you climb back into the car. "Where are we going?"

"You decide," you say. "I'm not a good tour guide for Los

Angeles. San Franciscans and Angelenos have a natural antipathy, kind of like Rome and Milano. I never visit L.A."

Perplexed, the professor looks around. "Well, how about Hollywood?"

You consult the map and make your way from freeway to freeway, rising above the endless blocks of low brick buildings with loud signs, crisscrossing the town. "Los Angeles is a *casino,*" the professor says, his voice full of admiration. *"Casino"* in Italian literally means "whorehouse," but Italians use the expression whenever they want to describe anything that is a big, unruly mess.

"Exactly," you say. The amorphous traffic amoeba you are in has decided to stop. No one in any of the other cars seems to notice, though, because they're all on their phones.

You finally exit to what says Hollywood on the map, park, and wander around some trashy lingerie shops, adult video arcades, and grimy convenience stores.

"How can this be Hollywood?" asks the professor. *"È bruttissima.* It's like Casablanca. It sounds much more glamorous than it is."

The professor suggests you head to Beverly Hills instead. He wants to explore some of the glitzy shops, to see how they compare with Paris. You are reluctant, since you aren't exactly dressed for shopping on Rodeo Drive. You are, in fact, never dressed for shopping on Rodeo Drive. "You are more refined than these people," the professor reassures you, looking around. "They have money but no taste."

The professor strides into a very expensive boutique with a French name, one you would never have dreamt of visiting, and looks around. The saleswoman, an impeccable size two, looks up from behind the counter and doesn't deign to notice you are there. "People don't greet you in stores the way they do in Italy," you whisper to the professor.

"Very rude." Despite the fact that he is dressed in jeans and a hippie vest, the professor summons up a very French air of hauteur. He flings his foulard around his neck and begins examining the clothing on the racks, arms crossed, head cocked, making comments. He greets the saleswoman in French, and when she answers, he winces at her French, and switches to English.

He breezes through the store, decides nothing is quite elegant, then samples a few bottles of perfume, making comments in French. One after another meets with his disdain. When he finds one that is all right, he applies a drop of perfume to the inside of your wrist, closes his eyes, and inhales.

"Troppo signora," he finally says, with a disappointed air. Too matronly. He sighs a you-just-can't-find-good-perfume-outside-of-Paris kind of sigh, and whispers to you that next time you're in Paris, you really ought to try a particular French brand that is much sexier. He nods to the saleswoman and you leave.

"Quite a performance," you say out on the sidewalk. "I've never seen you do a full Parisian."

"What do you mean?" he asks, feigning innocence. "There was nothing interesting in that shop. And the mademoiselle was *antipatica.*"

You like how he managed to out-snob the saleswoman with his innate elegance. You look him over.

"You know, one thing nice about you is that the clothes you brought with you are so economical," you tell him.

He fingers his shirt, looking a little hurt. "It's old," he says, "but not so cheap." He pulls on his tapestry vest. "I like my clothes."

You realize your language mistake. "I didn't mean economical as in inexpensive," you say. "I meant economical in the sense that you packed light, you brought just what you needed. I love the way you dress."

"Grazie."

Relieved, his vanity restored, you drive back to Santa Monica, where you had booked an elegant hotel right on the beach. The professor likes it even better when he finds out that as a travel writer, you've scammed the place for free. You are shown to your fresh green-and-white-shuttered room, with a view of the swimming pool and the ocean.

From your room, he walks out onto the little balcony and watches the sun go down over the ocean. "Wow," he says. He turns to you. "Not everyone has the chance to spend time like this, searching for pleasure. Not everyone recognizes the opportunity."

The professor hugs you. He changes into a fluffy white robe, runs a bath, lights a candle and a cigar, and then sinks into the hot Jacuzzi. He lies there silently for a while, soaking, and then motions you to join him in the tub. He draws in a deep puff of smoke and exhales luxuriously.

"I feel," he finally says, in English, "like Frank Sinatra."

In the morning, after breakfast on the terrace, you set off to explore museums. That was the main reason the professor wanted to visit L.A.; for all its faults, Los Angeles has plenty of world-class museums. The L.A. County Museum is closed, so you visit the Museum of Contemporary Art. You start with an exhibit of Nan Goldin's photographs, glimpses into disturbing private lives, move on through a retrospective of American modern art (the professor, impatient with all your questions, promises to explain everything from Giacometti to Rauschenberg on the drive home), and then you head off for the Getty Museum.

You drive from downtown to the sparse Santa Monica mountains, a hilltop setting overlooking the city grids. You take the tram up, above the city, with a view of the mountains and the ocean beyond. You arrive at a warm stone plaza with a shallow fountain that wets the bluish flowers of overhanging rosemary and ceanothus bushes. The professor is immediately impressed. You climb a broad staircase to the entrance hall and walk into the courtyard, with its fountains and potted native flowers. You study the buildings—rich, rough, warm blocks of Italian travertine with lighter, more transparent parts of the buildings in glass and tan metal, all of it visually stimulating and harmonious. The buildings seem timeless and permanent, a kind of modern Acropolis.

"Incredible," says the professor. "It is worth the trip to the United States just to see this architecture."

You go into some of the galleries, admire the light, and the ease with which you can move between the indoor and outdoor spaces on walkways, going from the collections to the courtyard. You pause on a balcony with a view of a promontory filled with barrel cactus, tall-armed saguaros, aloe, and other desert plants—all native to the place, but arranged in a wonderful graphic design. The whole campus is inviting and contemplative, and doesn't allow for the kind of fatigue that overwhelms you in most museums.

"Do you know who designed this museum?" asks the professor.

"Richard somebody?"

"Richard Meier," he says. "Everyone should know that name.

Forget about the paintings here, they are mostly second-rate paintings by first-rate artists, or first-rate paintings by second-rate artists. But the architecture is amazing, the building is an extraordinary work of art. This building will last for centuries."

You meander through the galleries, the professor walking briskly, pausing in front of only a few paintings—a lovely, delicate Flemish painting by Dieric Bouts called the *Annunciation* and a madonna by Fra Bartolomeo. You like the way the professor takes museums at the speed of his interest, his desires dictating the visit, not awed by the art, sluggishly viewing each piece, giving each the same authority and interest. He is in charge here, not the museum. He speeds through the French decorative arts, all that froth, studies a few tapestries, and then, into another gallery of paintings, comes to a full stop in front of one painting.

"This," he says, "is their best painting." It is *The Holy Family* by Nicolas Poussin, 1651. The professor begins gesturing at the painting, which depicts Jesus, Mary and Joseph, with the infant John and his mother Elizabeth, in a tranquil classical setting. "Look at the geometry of the background, the meticulous composition," he says, almost breathless. "Look at the delicate beauty of the faces, the expressions." Then he gestures to the drapery on the figures. "This is exquisite. The folds of the drapery are almost abstract, so ahead of his time. And the *colors*." He stands there without speaking for several minutes, gazing at the painting. "Yes," he murmurs, "a very beautiful Poussin. A masterpiece."

In his eyes, there is no use looking at any other paintings after that one, so you walk out to the gardens. You take a cool, tree-lined sandstone path that crosses a stream. The stream tumbles down to a terrace where fuchsia bougainvilleas climb up tall parasols of bent metal bars, spilling over like leaves on trees, and the water finally cascades down a stone wall into a reflecting pool filled with a maze of pink, red, and purple azaleas.

"Every detail is perfect," says the professor.

He sits under one of the bougainvilleas and smokes a cigarette, basking in the aesthetic pleasure of the place, all the senses soothed. "You're lucky to live so close to this," he says. "I may never see it again."

Unable to leave, you stay in the gardens until the museum closes, the last minute, and then head back to your swanky hotel. You swim, take a hot tub, and eat dinner at a nearby Asian-fusion restaurant. You talk about all the art you've seen that day. Halfway through dessert (the professor says you must always order dessert after a dinner of fish), he takes your hand and kisses it.

"You know," he says, "this isn't just a physical attraction between us. It's intellectual, too."

It's a sweet thing to say, a romantic moment, but in the back of your mind you think it has taken the professor an awfully long time to come to that revelation—or at least to say it out loud. You stroke one of his cheeks with your hand, and then kiss him on the other.

You wake up in the morning, make love with warm sunshine streaming in through the shutters, eat a breakfast in the hotel restaurant that costs about the same as a night in a cheap motel, and pack up your things. Settled in the convertible, he asks where you're going.

"A surprise," you say.

"You are full of surprises," he says. "Every day is another surprise, better and better." He adjusts his mirror and settles back for the ride. You go south on the freeway and exit into a neighborhood with lots of boxy tract houses and shopping malls near the beach.

"*Where* are we going?" he asks, confused.

"Be patient, my dear."

You make your way to an industrial port and finally park in an enormous lot surrounded by warehouses. "We're here," you say.

"Where?" he asks, looking around the godforsaken place.

"The boat. We're island specialists, and I promised you an island."

The professor beams. "An island!" he observes. "I forgot! The cherry on top of the cherry on top of the ice cream."

You buy tickets and board a boat for an island about an hour away. As you pull out, the professor looks around the port. "The strange thing about California," he observes, "is that you have all this coast, but you don't really have a sea culture."

"What do you mean?" you ask. "There's a beach culture, surfer culture, yachting culture . . ."

"It's not the same," he says. "Here, you play in the ocean, but only as an afterthought. This culture did not develop from the sea, from fishing, from boating trade. You can even tell by the cuisine."

True enough, you say. California was developed for its gold, not its mackerel. Then came Hollywood, agriculture, aerospace, and now the Internet frontier. No one ever made that big a deal out of the ocean. It's not like New England. People don't go around dressed like they just got off a boat.

"Bizarre," the professor murmurs, then heads to the front of the boat to put his face into the sun and breeze.

The sea is calm, with only a few sailboats ruffling the water. The island finally comes into view, round rugged hills hovering above the blue. The professor squints into the sun. "I don't see any buildings," he says. "Where are the hotels?"

"It's a nature preserve," you say. "There's only one hotel, a rustic place, and the rest is camping." You've never been to the place, so you have no idea what to expect.

"We're *camping*?" asks M., alarmed.

"Don't worry," you say. "We have a room."

Now you can see the soft, sandy beaches and mysterious coves, the wild, dry vegetation, and a handful of boats at the marina. It looks like a Mediterranean island. It is nowhere you would have found if you hadn't been searching for a perfect place to take the professor.

"This is incredible," M. says. "We are an hour off the coast of Los Angeles, and it looks like Greece. How can this exist?" He turns to face you. "Now I can never return to California, because nothing could ever compare to this." He takes your hand and squeezes it.

You disembark and a no-nonsense woman in a Jeep, a grown-up Girl Scout type, picks you up to take you to the simple lodge on the top of the hill. You've booked a room in the pretty inn, with a little balcony that has a view of both sides of the island and its narrow isthmus. The professor sits on the balcony in a prime tanning spot. "The Los Angeles hotel was a pleasure, a luxury, but this . . ." he lights a cigarette. "This is real, this is where you can truly relax. Who could imagine you could find this in the United States?"

He smokes and you watch the boats slowly move in and out of the marina. He is Mediterranean creature, and he is back on an island, completely in his element. "You know," he says, "in order for me to truly relax, I have to be outside my country, and even outside of my language. I can't relax in French."

"Why?" you ask.

He shrugs, and tries to explain. "If I speak French, I might as well be in France. There is an inherent nervousness. I have to get outside of it all."

You wonder out loud whether you are any different in Italian.

"You are softer in Italian," M. observes. "You're more all-business in English."

"Maybe," you say, "we can relax with each other because we don't speak each other's native language." It also helps that neither of you actually speaks Italian all that well. All the complicated negotiations and power games that usually go on in a relationship have to be simplified between you, each giving way, nothing ever serious. You can't speak the language well enough to be subtly cutting, hint at expectations or grievances, or infuse remarks with shades of meaning that might or might not be nasty, creating just enough maneuvering room in the words to plausibly pretend you aren't saying anything mean at all, your lover is just being paranoid. You can only be nice to each other; you can only concentrate on the present tense.

"Umm," he says, lifting up your shirt, sliding his fingers underneath. *"Molto rilassante."* Very relaxed.

The next morning, you leave after breakfast to explore the island. It is a brilliant day, no clouds, with a warm breeze. You stop at the one convenience store at the marina before setting out for a hike.

"We should bring some water and some food," you say. You have a little bit of Girl Scout in you, too, though you know better than to remind the professor not to forget his sunscreen and a hat.

"Maybe water," says the professor. "We can sit down to eat lunch when it's lunchtime." He makes a face at the processed snack items at the store.

"We might get hungry," you prompt, fingering a package of crackers. He gives you a look like, you Americans always have to have your snack foods, we French wait for a proper meal, and so you put it down. You buy a little bottle of water and leave.

You hike up a road that winds around the island's rugged coast. "Where are we going?" he asks.

"I don't know," you say. "I thought we could just take a hike."

"*Hike?*" says the professor. "That's so . . . *German.*"

"Okay, let's take a *walk.*"

You walk around a curve in the road, getting higher and higher above the ocean.

"Walking just to walk on this road isn't very interesting," the professor remarks, five minutes later. "It is only interesting if you go to a little beach where you can bathe."

"Then we'll walk to a little beach," you say.

"*Va bene,*" says the professor, content.

You are quiet for a while, and then the professor starts to talk about how he still can't believe he's visiting you in California, that it seemed so unlikely that you'd ever see each other again after Ischia.

"You thought it was impossible, that you couldn't write to me, that we wouldn't meet somewhere?" you ask.

"Well, you live so far away," he says, weighing his words. "And you could have met another man and forgotten all about me. And I, I had other obligations."

"Your family."

"The family, yes, but—" He kicks a pebble. "I almost wasn't able to meet you in Milano in May."

"Really? Why not?"

"Well, I had another plan."

"Ah, another woman."

He gives you a part sheepish, part devilish smile. "A brunette."

You nod. You aren't sure you want to hear about the brunette.

"It was such a surprise to meet you in Ischia," he says. "I was in the middle of another little story. You changed my plans. After that, I had to decide about my next vacation—the blonde or the brunette!"

You don't like, suddenly, to be reduced to your hair color. "So what happened to the brunette?"

The professor explains that the brunette is a Spanish academic, a professor of comparative literature, and they'd been seeing each other off and on for a while. He was supposed to meet her in Ischia, but she'd had to cancel at the last minute, something came up. Then he'd had a difficult year, he was depressed, and when they'd met again, instead of cheering him up, everything felt uncomfortable. It had all ended badly, and so he had decided to come see you in Milan instead.

You realize this kind of thing goes with the territory of having an affair with a married man. You can hardly be jealous, especially since he'd had a story with the brunette before he'd ever met you. You live a secret fantasy life together, and you have no right to expect anything. You keep telling yourself that.

"So I'm lucky. If things hadn't gone badly the last time you saw her I never would have seen you again," you say uneasily.

"Maybe not," says the professor. He glances at you, and can see there's some turbulence inside. "But I'm the one who is lucky, *cara*, especially since I know you better. When I met you in Ischia, I didn't realize you were so *spiritoso*, so witty."

"Just a silly American girl," you say. "Superficial, consumerist, McDonald's-eating . . ."

"Stop it," he says, serious. "I was trying to tell you how happy I am that I saw you again, how lucky I am. I would much rather be with you than a neurotic Spanish brunette." He stops walking and takes your hand. "You have given me a lot of energy. I'll never forget this trip."

You hike on, and around every curve is a steep cliff with a pristine, secluded, pocket beach below. There's just no way to get down there. "Maybe the next one," you say, and you walk on to the next curve, then the next, every beach enticing but impossible, until finally you find a beach that doesn't have quite as steep a cliff. You might be able to make it down. The professor is doubtful; it looks treacherous, there's no trail, and it's a long, crumbly slide to the bottom. But the beach is so inviting.

You start clambering down through the bushes, climbing over rocks and skidding down loose soil.

"We might be the first people in the world to make it to this beach," you say.

The professor, clutching a branch, peers up at you. "Do you think that once we get down there we'll be able to get back up?"

"If not, we can always swim."

You climb hand over foot down a steep rock face and then finally jump down the last rock onto the beach.

"We made it!" you say, exhilarated. The professor gives you a hug and you twirl around in the sand.

"Wonderful," he says. He finds a comfy place in the sand with a rock backrest, spreads out his towel, and motions you next to him. You take off your jeans and T-shirt, down to your shimmery underwear, and close your eyes.

"Don't think that just because you have your eyes closed, no one can see you," says the professor. He puts a hand on your warm stomach and you begin to make love, and in the back of your mind you think, this is the climax of the trip, making love in the sunshine on a secluded beach, and then rushing into the water afterward for a swim. After that, we'll be on our way back, on our way to the boat, back to L.A., back to San Francisco, back to Paris, the story finished, the end.

You stop thinking and make love hungrily, teasingly, and you climax together, shaking and then gasping at how strong it had been.

After lying, stunned, in the warm sand, you both get up and plunge into the ocean, the water so invigorating, so refreshing after sex. You float there, just staring at each other, not saying anything, for an endless moment.

Then, shivering, he swims back and you swim farther out. He calls out to be careful, pointing to something. A big mustachioed sea lion is doing sentry duty at the edge of your tiny cove. There's a mama sea lion with a pup on some rocks to the left. The father sea lion starts nosing his way toward you.

"Laura," says the professor, "come back now."

"Sea lions can't hurt you," you call back, not sure whether or not you're making that up. "They're just curious." Mr. Mustache is heading your way, blowing bubbles, more aggressive. You swim as hard as you can back toward the beach, until you're safely out of his territory.

The professor hands you a towel, a little peeved. "Stay closer," he says. "I don't want you to get hurt."

You put your clothes back on and you both realize at once

that you are hungry. The walk, the climb, the swim, the sex—you're ravenous. "You didn't bring those little biscuits, did you?" asks the professor. You nod no, mournfully. "And the water is gone?"

You climb back up the hill, easier than going down but still arduous, and finally make it to the top, brushing leaves and stickers off your clothes. You try hitchhiking, but absolutely no cars are circling the island, so you set off on foot. The walk back is much, much longer than the walk there.

"Maybe," says the professor, carefully considering it, "you were right about bringing the biscuits." He has just made an amendment to French protocol, pronouncing that it is admissible to snack under the circumstance of being stranded in a wild place that is so uncivilized as to not have a proper restaurant or even supplies for *le pic-nique*.

Two hours later, famished and thirsty, you fall upon the grocery store, buy crackers and processed cheese, and sit down with an American canned beer. An immense feeling of relief and well-being comes over you after you eat, and you go down to the beach and nap. You take a final swim in the marina, knowing it will be your last ocean swim for who knows how long. The water has a distinct chill to it; the September summer is turning to fall.

You eat a fish dinner when the one restaurant opens, fresh grilled shark with the works—French fries, French dressing—and wait for the boat. You board, taking a seat on the outside deck, and stare at the stars as the boat pulls away from the island. You put your head on the professor's lap. You know that your perfect day, your perfect vacation, is coming to an end. It's all highways home from here. He will be leaving, and you will be alone again. You're starting to get used to having him around. You try not to let the professor see your tears.

"You know, my dear," he says, stroking your hair. "It isn't a bad thing to always know that someone on the other side of the world cares about you, that someone is always thinking about you with pleasure."

When you make it back to the parking lot and the convertible, it's already late. It's going to be a long drive home.

"The *dénouement*," you say, slaughtering the pronunciation.

The professor corrects you. "What do you mean by that?" he asks.

"It's a literary term, no? It means the long slide after the climax to the ending, when everything gets resolved."

"It means the untangling, but we don't use it to talk about books."

As you start back toward San Francisco, you get that awful feeling of having to crash back into reality when you've been floating in paradise. You put on the Rolling Stones, loud and energetic, to stay aloft. You come up over a hill and suddenly all of Los Angeles is spread out before you, an endless glory of neon lights.

"Wonderful," says the professor. The music, the lights, the Los Angelesness of it all—he loves it. The professor always manages to find his own personal zing of pleasure even in the most unlikely places. The delight that you always experience traveling together, you realize, is something that you both actually carry around with you. That makes you feel better about leaving the island, about him leaving you soon.

You drive and drive, the professor smoking, happy, chattering away, until you're too tired to drive any more. You pull off at a highway exit with motel signs.

"Cheap motel," you say. "The true American experience." It's about two in the morning, and a snoozy clerk hands you a room key. You find your way to your room, with its orange bedspread, razor blade-sized bars of soap, and warnings about not stealing the towels.

"It's not a *hotel du charm*," you say, "but there's something sexy about a cheap motel. It's kind of anonymous and illicit, like you could be sleeping with a stranger."

"Hmmm," says the professor, testing the mattress. You fall into bed, ready to sleep immediately. The professor takes his time, brushing his teeth, folding his shirt, placing it into his suitcase. He slides under the covers and puts a hand on your bottom, stroking you.

"What did you say your name was, *mademoiselle*?" he says.

"Mmmph," you say, curling away from him.

"That's okay," he says, "I can make love to you while you're asleep. You just lie there and dream that you're making love to a sexy stranger." He begins exploring your body, making comments in French. You start to wake up. Suddenly you are having sex with an anonymous French man. It's exciting and quick; it comes out of nowhere.

"*Ça va, mademoiselle?*" he says in French.

"*Oui, monsieur.*"

He lies back on the pillows. "Cheap motel," he says, in English. "I like it."

You make good time the next morning, driving north on Highway 101 while the professor, as promised, lectures about art. "Art history 101," you say. You skip impressionism, because you both agree that secretly you think impressionism is *troppo dolce,* a little too sweet. He runs through modernism, symbolism, Vuillard, Bonnard, German Expressionism, Cubism, Chagall, and Rousseau before you stop to pee. After that, diet cola and sparkling water in hand, you pass over Dada and surrealism, do minimalism minimally, and then exit to abstract expressionism, the most American of modern art. The professor is crazy about Barnett Newman, with his big color-field paintings with the stripes down the middle.

"So why," you ask, "isn't Barnett Newman a minimalist?"

"Good question, *signorina*," he says, adopting his professorial air. "The difference is that Barnett Newman is sublime."

"Art people always say 'sublime.' What do you *mean* by sublime?"

The professor sighs. Newman's paintings are mystical, he says, the austerity of the image and the intensity of the single line create a unity of opposites; the paintings create an immediate, spiritual experience when the viewer enters into the luminous color space. "And the zip!" exclaims the professor. "The zip!" He goes into the anthropology of the zip's verticality, whatever that is, how Newman's zip is like the statues of Giacometti, that both speak to the condition of man, man distinguished from animals. The fundamental condition of man is his verticality— the zip, the tall skinny statues—both artists reduce man to his essence.

"And Rothko?"

"Ah, Rothko," says the professor. "Matisse is beautiful. Newman is sublime. But Rothko—Rothko is beautiful *and* sublime!"

"Rothko *rules*," you say.

"Rothko *forever*," he says, slipping playfully into your American slang. You drive on in silence for a while.

"*E allora?*" you ask. Now what?

"Well," he says, "we could talk about sex."

"If we *talk* about sex any more," you say, "you won't want to *have* sex any more."

He considers that. "But there's one thing we haven't discussed," he says.

You raise a querying eyebrow.

"Masturbation!"

"Professor," you say, "what kind of a discourse are you going to make on masturbation? The verticality of the zip?"

"That is really stupid," he says, suppressing a laugh.

"How about," you say, looking over at him, "if I just watch?"

"Watch what?"

"Watch you."

"Watch me what?"

"You know. I'm bored driving here. How about if I watch you, you know."

The professor reddens. *"Impossible!"*

"Come on, it would be beautiful *and* sublime."

The professor crosses his legs, clearly a bit uncomfortable.

"I've succeeded in embarrassing a Frenchman about sex. Who'll ever believe it," you say.

"No, no, not embarrassed," he says, folding his arms. "It just isn't . . . *comme il fait.*"

"It just isn't done?"

"No, *mademoiselle.*"

"Un peccato," you say. A shame. "Okay, then, so tell me about Rauschenberg."

It is still sunny when you arrive in San Francisco, remarkably, and you head toward the Haight, taking a back route over Twin

LAURA FRASER

Peaks. You wind around the hills and then park at the vista point, where the entire city, from the Golden Gate Bridge clear south to Candlestick Park, is spread out before you.

The professor gasps at the view. "Another surprise," he says. "I thought there were no more surprises."

"There's always another surprise."

You get back into the car, and he turns to you. "You know, these have been the twelve most beautiful days of my life."

"Seriously?" you say. You're so pleased. You'd been to some wonderful places together, but it was dawning on you that you could feel happy with the professor almost anywhere. You were growing together. You couldn't tell him that, though; he might worry that you would start calling him in Paris in the middle of the night.

"I mean it. When I get home it will all seem like a dream."

You spend the afternoon unpacking, only for him to pack again, all the rituals of leave-taking. You make love, shower, and get dressed.

"You know," he says, looking you over, "you are much prettier after you have had sex. Your whole face is relaxed."

"After this vacation, I should look good for a while."

"Una piccola riserva," he says. "A little reserve, until you meet someone else."

You drive to Berkeley to your favorite restaurant, a small café with simple food made of exquisite ingredients, a place you've splurged on only a few times, very special occasions. The last time you were here was the day after your husband had left you for good, when you learned that even under the worst conditions there's nothing like a fabulous meal with a friend, finished

126

off with a flaky rhubarb tart with Valencia orange ice cream, to cheer you up.

Sitting at that restaurant once again with the professor, you realize you don't really need such a good meal at all. You already feel full; after twelve days with him, your senses are saturated. That moment of pleasure you'd let in that evening at the restaurant the evening after your husband left you, that crack in your depression, had widened with the professor's help, and you don't think it will close again, even after he leaves. Still, you enjoy the meal thoroughly, the snobbish Parisian admitting he has never tasted beef like that before in his entire life.

The next morning, before leaving, the professor goes to a music store and buys some of the CDs you played for him on the road, to remember the trip. He also finds a Serge Gainsbourg CD for you, and plays a song. It's kind of cheesy, with Jane Birkin panting amorously with Serge, cooing over and over, *je t'aime . . . moi non plus.*

"Do you understand the words?" asked the professor.

"Well, mainly," you say, uncertain.

"They're words I can't say," he says.

I love you; me neither. He loves you, but of course he can't express it directly. But for that moment—that bite, that painting, those twelve days—you are floating together in the intensity of the present, of pleasure, of love. It doesn't matter that he lives on the other side of the world and is married and a real relationship isn't possible. It's real enough.

To distract you from the tension of leaving, of words you can't say, you have dinner with your Italian-speaking friend Cecilia, who met the professor the week before—only the week before?—in your garden. You tell her the story of your trip, and she brings out a dictionary, serenely looking up the correct Italian for words you've been using together that, apparently, you've made up.

Your espressos are finished; it's time to catch the plane. You each kiss Cecilia good-bye and drive to the airport in silence. You pull up to the curb at the airport and help him unload his little bag.

"This is the terrible part," he says. You blink and smile, avoiding looking at him directly.

"But it isn't the end of the story," he says. "We'll see each other again. Where and how, I don't know. But I'm sure of it."

He unwraps his Egyptian scarf and holds it out to you. "I want you to have this."

You refuse. "That's your favorite piece of clothing. You wear it all the time. No one will recognize you without that."

"That's what makes it a good gift." He places it around your neck. "You can hang it in your bedroom and think about me."

"Thank you," you say, hugging it around you.

You kiss and hold on to each other for a long time, your tears wetting his shoulder. Then another quick peck on each cheek, *ciao, ciao*, and you quickly drive away.

SEVEN

LONDON

The professor had, in fact, left you with *una piccola riserva*. It helped you stay calm over the next few months, less frantic about the idea that you were single, childless, nearing forty, and might never meet a man who would look you in the eyes and tell you how lucky he was to meet you, how much he loves your smile, how alive you make him feel.

Your friends say you'll find the guy, it just takes time to get over a heartbreak. Different friends have different theories: some say it takes a year; others, the amount of time you were together with your ex. But you have serious doubts. You're wary of falling in love again anyway. Love has caused you too much trouble in the past. You aren't even sure if it was ever really love to begin with, or just a projection of narcissism, the delight of seeing your idealized self reflected in someone else. It doesn't matter. All those bright, soft moments of falling in love are buried by divorce now, under shovelfuls of shit, and it's hard to know whether they can ever be excavated again as pleasant memories.

You're going to use your reserve to keep your distance, to take what the Italians call *una pausa*. To give it a rest. You stop searching for a replacement husband, stop computer dating, and stop looking for that intelligent, witty, kind, sexy man who shares at least a few of your passions. If he's out there, you figure, he's already married anyway, or else there's something psychotically wrong with him. So there's no rush.

Friends of yours, even the seemingly happily married ones, hint that having a French lover you see every six months or so might actually be the perfect relationship. You have time for your busy life, your career, your friends, your yoga and Italian classes, and then every so often you can go somewhere exotic and immerse yourself in sex and romance. You don't have to deal with all of the little disappointments that relationships inevitably bring, and you never take each other for granted. Your expectations are never dashed because there is no possibility that the relationship can ever be more than it is, a sometime affair thousands of miles away.

Still, you know you want more. You grew up believing in the happily-ever-after scenario. Far from understanding, after Jon left you, that expectations can poison a relationship, you cling to the fantasy of finding a perfect husband. Once marriage becomes the defining narrative in your life, it's hard to go back to a different story. You can't return to being defiantly, happily single. Now you're unmarried, divorced. You've failed at marriage, in some eyes—even your own—and you feel incomplete without a man, all of which makes it that much more difficult to try casual dating again. You feel completely unmoored around men, never sure what is stable.

You realize this after having a drink one evening with a man from one of your Italian classes, a warm and intelligent Italo-

American historian you consider a new friend, someone with whom it would be fun to practice Italian. This friend surprises you first by kissing you and telling you he's attracted to you, then by explaining that he's married, with children. It's a kind of love-less marriage, he says, they stay together for the kids. He wants to have a fling with you, erotic adventures in the afternoons, that sort of thing. You tell him you're sorry, but what is there for you in that scenario? You're bound to want more and be disappointed. You can't imagine a relationship where you can't wake up in the same bed as your lover.

"Perhaps," he tells you, "you are the type of woman who lives from affair to affair, who travels the world and always finds a new passion."

Perhaps. And it doesn't sound so bad, the kind of life where you end up wearing fabulous hats in your sixties and recounting your many affairs to your women friends over lunch. But you wonder if it would be lonely in the end.

So you take a little *pausa*. You think about the professor occasionally, warmly, but try not to dwell on him—even if you are sometimes tempted to call him up just to hear his deep, rich voice.

A couple of weeks after he left San Francisco, he sends you a postcard, Man Ray's photo of tears, telling you, "It was a moment of glory, of pleasure, and of beauty that I can't forget . . . I hope for another chapter in this life . . . hugs, M."

That, at least for the moment, *is* enough.

In February, you are invited on a press trip to Egypt. You've never taken a press tour before, because you've always figured it's more fun to discover things for yourself when you're traveling than to have them "discovered" for you, in advance. The chance encounters you have on a group trip usually all happen on the first day, and then you're stuck with them. But you can hardly resist a free trip to Egypt, with a stopover in London.

You write to the professor and ask if he can see you that weekend. He telephones to arrange the details, all business, and then writes you a postcard later, saying that when he heard your voice and thought about you there in your monumental bed, it gave him a terrible desire to make love. That, he says, is why he hates talking on the phone.

You go on the two-week trip—a whirlwind of monuments, museums, tombs, luxury hotels, a cruise up the Nile, and a bus ride through the Sinai—and when it's over, you land in London, which is cool and Technicolor green after Cairo. By then, you're glad to leave the group of travel writers. London on your own actually seems more exotic than Egypt on a tour.

The boutique hotel you've booked is in a Mary Poppins district of London. The hotel has a Victorian feel, an English-colonial version of Egypt. You put on the gold and black embroidered robe you bought in a market by the side of the Nile, stretch out under the regally maroon canopy bed, and wait for the professor. You have a glass of wine to calm your jittery anticipation. The receptionist finally phones to tell you, in a prim voice, that you have a visitor.

You open the door, and there he is, hardly recognizable in a conservative blue sport jacket and tweed overcoat, looking every bit a Londoner, which hardly looks like him. The professor drops his things and plops onto the bed. He reaches for you and you are making love before you even have a chance to quite grasp that he is there. It feels more like a dream of the past than the present. You lie there quietly for a few minutes, and he goes to take a bath. He returns in a robe, refreshed, looking more like himself, and pours himself a glass of wine.

"Not bad," he says, taking in the oriental surroundings. "Not bad at all to be met by a pretty woman, naked under her Egyptian robe, in an exotic bed." He sits back down on the bed, against the pillows. "I feel like a pasha."

You are excited to be with him; you have so much to show and tell. You pull out a scarf you found for him in the market in Aswan. He's pleased, admires the color, and wraps it around his neck. You show him the photos of your trip to California, and he is delighted—the professor in a convertible in front of a palm tree, the view from the top of Twin Peaks in San Francisco. "I was so tan," he sighs, his vanity never far from the surface.

You have come to the point with each other where you can talk about your past, nostalgic. It's a deeper, and maybe more ordinary, kind of intimacy.

"I told all my friends three things," says the professor. "You must see the Getty Museum, San Francisco is a beautiful city, and there is no sea culture in California."

"And what else stays with you, professor?"

"Seeing the lights of Los Angeles at night while we were playing the Rolling Stones," he says. "And the two strongest times we made love."

"Which two?"

"Guess."

"On the beach on the island and the night in the cheap hotel."

"Exactly," he says.

"They were both in the same day," you say.

"*Incredibile,*" he says, and glances down at his zipper. "You are making *Lui,* him, excited again. You are terrible."

You make love again, but this time you feel like he is right there with you, right then.

You leave the hotel and walk to an Indian restaurant for dinner.

"*Raccontami, cara,*" he says, after you've sat down. "Tell me about your trip."

It was wonderful to be in Egypt, you tell him, to see the temples and tombs, to cruise up the Nile from Aswan to Luxor, to visit camel traders and souks, and to have a very learned Egyptologist along who could read hieroglyphs and tell tales about the Egyptian gods. From the point of view of seeing the ancient art and understanding it better, it was amazing.

You are suddenly relieved to be with someone, maybe the only one, who understands your travel sensibility. "My roommate on the trip," you say, finally able to voice a complaint, "brought *nine* pairs of shoes." Your packing philosophy is that you should always be able to run *with* your luggage; hers was that the bellboy should always be able to run *for* your luggage.

"*Mon dieu,*" says the professor.

"The people in the group wanted so much comfort. They wanted to feel like they were in an American hotel, and they'd get upset when anything wasn't up to standard. They didn't seem to grasp that we were in Egypt, not a Hilton hotel in Cincinnati."

"Well," says the professor, "you were on a tour." He would rather spend two weeks in a Parisian prison than go on an organized tour.

But aside from all that, there were many great moments, you tell him. "I celebrated my birthday there."

"Happy birthday," says the professor. "What are you—thirty-four?"

"Something like that."

It had been a magical evening, a dinner in Cairo. Your Egyptian guide presented you with roses, and as the birthday girl, you had to get up and belly dance. Having a belly, it turns out, is necessary but not sufficient for belly dancing, but you did your best. Then a fortune-teller read your coffee grounds. She peered at you, and after reviewing your recent romantic life with remarkable clarity—you have suffered a great loss recently, but you will see that you are just getting rid of extra baggage—she gave you some advice: Forget about all those men in the past, stop worrying about men who aren't truly interested in you, and wait for a good one to fall in love. And she left you with another piece of advice. "Live each day of your life fully," she said.

"Giusto," says the professor. That's right. He clicks glasses of beer with you. "And so where do you think you'll be on your next birthday?" he asks.

"Who can say," you say. "Not Egypt."

You break the thin crisp *pappadams* and dip them into spicy sauces. "Who says the English don't have good food?" asks the professor.

He sips his beer, and asks you where else you went. The professor loves hearing about Egypt—he lived in Cairo as a child, where his father was a political prisoner—but he doesn't talk about that time in his life much. You tell him you also went to the Sinai peninsula for a couple of days.

It was strange, how it had changed since you were there on a trip after college, when you traveled with a backpack throughout the Mediterranean for nine months. Then, you'd taken an impromptu camel safari with some Bedouins you'd run into—

an astonishing, otherworldly trip into the interior of the Sinai mountains—and ended up in Sharm al-Sheikh, a village on the tip of the Sinai peninsula, where a few hippies and scuba divers had found an underwater paradise. So it was very unsettling, you tell the professor, to fly into Sharm al-Sheikh's airport sixteen years later. There were billboards, casinos, discos, golf resorts, and a four-lane highway. Your group excursion one day was to a Bedouin camp that had been set up for tourists, where you rode a camel for three minutes, and then drank tea before boarding the bus back to the resort hotel.

The professor crushes a cigarette in the ashtray. "When you go to a place and have an extraordinary experience," he says, "you can never return."

"That's true."

"I could never return to Ischia," he says.

"No," you agree. "Never."

In the morning, you wake up curled around each other. You have slipped right back into the intimacy of deep sleep.

"I don't understand it," says the professor, leaning back against the pillows after you make love.

"What?"

"Why is it so much better?" he asks, confused.

"Why is *what* so much better?"

"The sex."

"What sex?"

"This sex," he says.

"Better than?"

"Nothing," he says. He pauses, and a sly grin spreads across his face. *"Una giovane studentessa."* The professor explains that while he would never sleep with one of his students, he did have a little story with an ex-student. It was a complete surprise to him, but she had kept flirting with him—

"How old?" you ask.

"I don't know," he says, rolling over to reach for his pack of cigarettes. "Maybe nineteen."

You shake your head. You could live without hearing about his fling with a nineteen-year-old. You're part of his secret life, and he likes to share stories about his secret life, but you want to be special. The truth about the professor is that he needs a friend to talk to as much as he needs a fling every now and then. Friendship is more intimate for him than sex. But *nineteen*?

"You are a real Humbert Humbert," you say. "Pretty soon, I'm going to be too old for you."

"Dai," he says. "It has nothing to do with age. Anyway, the story is closed. She had some boyfriend problem."

"So let me get this straight," you say, sitting up in bed. "You don't understand how the sex could be better with me than with her?"

"Non ha senso," he says. It makes no sense.

"How about," you say, "the fact that I'm *twice* her age and I've been having sex since she was *born*."

The professor considers that. "Could be."

You cross your arms. "Then there's the possibility that since we've now known each other for a while, and shared many intimate moments—adventures, even—maybe *that* makes the sex better," you say.

He seems deep in thought.

"You know, the truth is, she really was too thin," he says. "And too young."

You roll your eyes. The professor is clearly trying to placate you.

"No, really," he says. "I'm not just saying that. It's true."

You start getting up out of bed.

"Anyway," he says, lightly slapping you on the behind, "the sex with you *is* much better."

"Non c'è dubbio, professore," you say. You have no doubt about that. You aren't worried about being less interesting company than a nineteen-year-old.

You order breakfast and eat it in bed.

Over croissants, you tell the professor—since you are sharing your secret lives, and since you are a little sore about the nineteen-year-old—about a man you met at a bar the month before. You weren't interested in him—he was too short and old for you, but he made you laugh.

"How old?" asks the professor.

"Nearing fifty," you say.

"That is not so old," he says. Just about his age.

Anyway, you say, you had a few drinks with this guy, who turned out to be a writer, and over the next few days, you made inquiries among a few writer friends. San Francisco is a rather small town. In short time, you found out that he was an accomplished, if eccentric writer, that he was an awful lot of fun to be with, and that he was a constant womanizer. "He seemed sort of taken with me," you told someone who knew him fairly well. "Do you think I'm special?"

"Oh, you're special, all right," the friend said. "They're *all* special."

The professor smiles.

You read two of his books, out of curiosity, got caught up in his character, and then invited him to a high-spirited party, where everyone drank too much and flirted recklessly. You were wearing your bronze Italian top, in keeping with the be-sexy-for-yourself divorcée philosophy, and the writer couldn't keep his hands off you. You told him to behave, and he offered you a ride home, very gentlemanly, and then he took you to his house for a drink, where the two of you didn't behave at all.

"So?" the professor asks.

"I realized he wasn't nearly as nice or interesting as the character he'd made himself out to be in his books." He'd never asked you a thing about yourself; you were just a dame, and in the morning, he could barely take the time to make coffee for you.

"Did you see him again?" asks the professor.

You wish you could tell him no. But somehow, a month later, after ignoring you, the writer convinced you to go skiing with him. You flew down the mountains together, exhilarated.

"We had fun for a day, but that's it," you say. "The truth is that I didn't trust the guy."

"Well," the professor says, whisking some crumbs off the sheets. "If it becomes *una storia,* don't tell him about your secret life."

You take the Underground to Hyde Park, where the air is fresh, there's a crocus or two pushing up, and it feels good to move and stretch at your own pace. You come upon a small museum, the Serpentine, and look at some large-scale photographs there, by Andreas Gursky.

"The interesting thing here," says the professor, after glancing around the exhibit, "is the relationship of his photos to painting." He stands in front of one photograph. "This one refers to a nineteenth-century landscape by Friedrich."

That, of course, hasn't occurred to you. You never like art

that is an inside joke, where you have to know the reference or else you can't appreciate what you're looking at—although that photo, by itself, as a landscape, is beautiful. "What other paintings does he comment on?" you ask. You might as well make use of the art professor.

He casts about the gallery. "This one," he says, standing in front of a photo of a river, *Rhein*. "What does this photo remind you of?" he asks.

It makes you uncomfortable when the professor quizzes you. You're sure you're a bad student. "I like the tension between the real image and the abstract composition," you say, stalling for time. The river makes a vertical line in a horizontal landscape that looks like an abstract color field. You take a stab at it. "Barnett Newman," you say. "The verticality of the zip!"

"Brava," says the professor. "It is not so difficult, hmmm? You just have to be willing to have a conversation with a work of art."

That evening, you have dinner at the hotel, a hidden cellar dining room, very chic.

"This place," you tell the professor, "is known for being a place where people have illicit affairs."

"So we fit right in," he says. But you don't: the restaurant is too self-consciously formal. You are better off in an Indian or Middle Eastern restaurant. But the professor is wearing a jacket, and you have on a black travel dress that goes anywhere, with the right scarf, so you fake it together. You're a team. The food is good, the kind of nouvelle cuisine you can get at any of a hundred San Francisco restaurants, no big deal unless you think presentation counts for a lot. The atmosphere is clubby, with big, gilt-edged floral paintings.

"Tell me," says the professor, diving into the serious, intimate conversation that goes with the place, "what has happened with your divorce?"

"It's over," you say. "Papers signed, completely finished. I am officially a divorcée."

"*Cin cin*," he says, clinking glasses with you. He settles back into his chair. "And so, are *you* over it, *signorina*?"

You twirl your glass. "I'm more or less over *him*," you say. "I don't think about him much, and I don't really miss him."

"*Va bene*," says the professor. "Have you seen him since?"

"No." In December, you say, you got a phone call from him, to talk about taxes. He was all business, but it upset you to hear his voice after so many months. He told you he wished you well, and that if you ever wanted to talk, he would be available. You thanked him and hung up. Talk about what? Talk about how things are going in his new house with his new girlfriend? Talk about how you may be over him, but you're not over getting your heart broken? About how he taught you that you couldn't trust true love at all, and because of that, you couldn't trust yourself? Talk about how, after four years with him and a few years to recover, there's no time left for you to have a child? Talk about what.

"I'm over him, but I'm not over the whole divorce. It takes awhile to be calm again with men, not to be neurotic."

"That's natural," the professor says.

"I regret the time I spent with him," you say. Your marriage just feels like a big black hole in your life. You spent four years in that hole, and then emerged back where you had started, as if none of it had ever happened. It was like a *Twilight Zone* episode. When you came back, you lived with a roommate again, did the same work, had the same friends, almost as if your husband had never existed. You don't know any of his friends or family any-more. The only person you've remained close to is his grand-mother, because you enjoy seeing her, and she's had the grace to remain friends with you. The rest of the four years are lost.

"You can't regret a whole period in your life like that," says the professor. "It may have ended badly, but when you were in love, you were in love. You learned something from him, from being together, and from getting divorced. It's a part of who you are, one of your stories."

He looks at you and nods, assuring you it's true, and then picks up his knife and fork and cuts into his meat.

"I guess you're right." You consider that. There were, actually, a lot of authors you never would've read if you hadn't met your husband—Robertson Davies, Paul Auster, Vikram Seth, Julian Barnes. You might not have picked up Dickens or John Irving again, either. What else? You learned that it was easy, frighten-ingly easy, to get lost in someone else's life, accommodating him, and stop being yourself. You learned to be wary about falling in love. And you learned that someone who had loved you could stop loving you, for some dark reason, and even though that was bruising, you were more resilient than you knew. Eventually you would get over it, more or less.

The professor concentrates on his meal.

"The thing I regret is not so much the relationship," you say, "as the time." Those four years, in your mid-thirties, were pre-cious ones. "I don't have much time left to have children," you tell him.

"Children," says the professor. "You can't plan children. I never thought about having children. They just came."

You nod. You both are quiet for a moment. "Can you imagine me as a father?" asks the professor. He puts on a sophisticated, rakish pose, but you can see through it. You can picture him being very soft-hearted and playful with his kids.

"I'm sure you're a good father," you say, serious. In fact, it had crossed your mind that he might make a good sperm-donor–type father, too. It would be lovely to have a little quarter-Italian, quarter-Arab child, a child from a romantic island encounter. Maybe they would even see each other from time to time.

"Thank you," he says. He takes a few more bites. "Have you thought about having a baby by yourself?" he asks.

You smile. "Everyone asks me if I'm going to adopt a kid from China," you say. "Right after the divorce, people started mentioning it, as if I should've been off making plane reservations to Beijing. Or they ask if I've considered freezing my eggs, or finding a gay man to raise a child with. Or they suggest that maybe I should just have a one-night stand with a reasonably intelligent man after ascertaining that he doesn't have a family history of mental illness."

"And?" asks the professor.

"It's too much," you say. "I'm independent, I travel, I don't have a lot of money. Plus, I'm not a very patient person. How am I going to raise a child by myself? If you decide to have a child with a partner, and it doesn't work out, that's one thing. Then you're a single mother. You deal. But you don't plan to be a single mom."

The professor makes a gesture like, well, whatever suits you.

"The main thing," you say, "is it wouldn't be fair to the baby. A baby needs a father, or at least another parent, another person to bounce things off of. They need someone else to give them love and guidance."

"You know," says the professor, listening to you, "I actually think you would be a good mother."

"Thank you," you say, and you continue eating your meal. "We'll see."

You order coffee, and then a grappa, for you. The professor inhales the aroma, but you drink most of it.

"I think one of the biggest tragedies," muses the professor, "would be to have a child that you didn't know about, or that you couldn't be a father to."

You wonder if he suspects that you had been fantasizing about that little quarter-Italian kid with a nice Mediterranean first name—maybe Marco, Dante, Lia, or Roma.

"That would be terrible," you say.

"*Sì,*" he says. "*Molto triste.*"

"*Triste,*" you repeat.

The next morning, you go to the Tate Gallery. He strides through at his usual pace, stopping in front of only a couple of the Turners, the ones that are clearly the most beautiful. You are too worn out for the National Portrait Gallery, so you decide to walk around Hampstead instead.

You wander into a small cemetery to look at the grounds, the old stone tombstones covered in vines, with a wrought iron fence and a solid little church.

"What's going to happen when you die, professor?" you ask.

"Now *that* I don't know, *signorina,*" he says. "I am a professor of art, not theology."

"I mean, what do you want done with your body?"

The professor frowns. He says he already has a cemetery plot. Or maybe, he says, he'll give his body to science.

"Do you imagine they'd be interested in your brain?" you ask. "Or *Lui,*" glancing at his trousers.

He shakes his head at you, not deigning to answer.

"I'm going to be cremated," you say.

The professor shudders. "I don't want to make anyone I love have to deal with those ashes," he says.

"It's not so bad," you say. "Although there are more big chunks than you'd expect."

"This is a morbid conversation," he says.

"Okay," you say, and you keep walking quietly. "Listen," you say, stopping. "Would you let one of your friends know about me, give him your address? Just in case something happens to you?"

The professor looks at you in disbelief. "I'm not dead yet," he says.

"I didn't mean . . ." you say. "Really, you're not even that old." You're making it worse. But it has crossed your mind that if you suddenly never heard from the professor again, you wouldn't know what happened, whether he'd just found a new lover, or whether he was dead. He does smoke an awful lot of cigarettes. You just want to know. He wasn't someone, anymore, who could just disappear from your life. "Just tell someone, okay?" you ask. You're nearing tears.

The professor stops and looks at you. "Okay, Laura," he says. "Okay."

That evening, you are taking a bath in the big claw-footed tub, when the professor comes in to inspect his face in the mirror. You are both uncomfortably aware that he has a train early in the morning, and that your short weekend is nearly over.

"And so," he says, making small talk, "what romantic prospects do you have when you return?"

"None." You are getting a little tired of talking about the men, or lack of men, in your life. It isn't something you are as worked up about as you used to be.

"Come on," he says. "You must have something simmering on the back burner."

You sigh. "No one seems to be interested at the moment. I don't know why. Maybe I'm too much for a lot of men."

"You are a little fat," he says.

"That's not exactly what I meant," you say, standing up in the tub. You motion to the professor to hand you a towel, and get out, drying yourself off. "The thing is," you tell the professor, wrapping the towel around your hair, "I have a very intelligent body."

"What do you mean, intelligent?" asks the professor. "There's no such thing as an intelligent body."

"Sure there is," you say. "I'm athletic, flexible, I can dance, ski, do a handstand . . ."

"Flexibility is good," the professor concedes.

You find a brush and begin to untangle your hair. "I may not have a fashionable body, but painters all through history would have loved it. It's womanly." You walk back out into the bedroom.

He sits next to you on the bed and puts a hand on your thigh. "Well, not all artists," he says. "Not Modigliani. Not Giacometti. Not El Greco."

You flick away his hand with the brush.

"Well, maybe Rubens."

"Rubens," you say, "give me a break. I'm no Rubens, and I'm no Botero, either."

He puts his arm around your waist to pull you toward him

and you push him away. "Name some painters who would have painted me, Monsieur art professor."

"Okay," he says, acting like he's making a big effort. "Tiziano." Again, you push him away. "Four more, professor," you say, "or forget it."

He sighs and looks at your body anew. "Courbet," he says, running his hand along your thigh. You skid away and count one on your finger. He thinks. "Renoir." You count two. You tap your two fingers softly on his leg. "Ingres, and Boucher," the professor says. He makes a move to touch you again.

"One more," you demand playfully. "One more who's French."

"You said four."

"I changed my mind."

"Okay, okay," he says. "Poussin."

"Bravo, professor." And then you let him touch you.

You sleep deeply. In the morning, while you are only half awake, he gives you a kiss on the cheek and slips out the door.

EIGHT

THE AEOLIAN ISLANDS

When you return to San Francisco, you feel sad. It isn't just that letdown that comes after any vacation, when you have to throw out the bad milk, do the laundry, and get back to the dull business of figuring out how to make enough money to pay the rent and start saving for your next trip. It's more a sense of loss. Every time you leave the professor, you come home feeling more alone than ever. If you're by yourself all the time, you get used to it; after awhile you don't notice the absence of someone sleeping next to you. But if you spend a few days here and there cuddling up with someone you care about, the fact of your aloneness becomes that much more obvious when you return to your own bed.

You begin seeing more of the writer, partly to escape that feeling of loss. Better to be with someone who is fun and distracting, even if he isn't a good long-term prospect, than to be by yourself. Maybe you are ready to date casually after all. And you do have fun with him: playing music together, in-line skating, skiing, going to concerts, parties, restaurants. He is a verbal gymnast who makes you laugh. So what if he doesn't reliably return phone calls or remember dates, never has enough cash to pay for anything, is cagey about mysterious engagements, strikes your friends as overly flirtatious, always wants to play lead guitar while you back him on piano, and tries to dissuade you from writing a book (*he's* the real writer). One day he asks you when you're going to take down the photo of "that French guy" in your office and put up one of him. You avoid his question and quickly change the subject.

Occasionally you muse that the writer is so much fun, you could end up in a real relationship. People change. He could grow up, become more responsible. After all, he's only forty-nine. You wonder if a day will come when you'll have to tell the professor that you can't have another *rendez-vous* with him, that maybe you should just have lunch or something the next time you are in Paris.

You write the professor a postcard and mention that you are having a little story with someone. You don't like hearing about his affairs, but it seems to make him happy to know that you are seeing someone else. He wants you to enjoy yourself, not pine away, and particularly not pine away for him. "I hope we can find each other again in September," he writes back, "if your new 'husband' lets go of you. It seems to me you have found someone who holds on to you tight, and doesn't want you to leave. If that's the case—lose him!" He adds a postscript, saying that after London, next time you have to find somewhere more exotic to meet.

You aren't sure when that will be.

You spend more and more time with the writer. You take a trip together, hiking around the red rock country in southern Utah, the area your husband and you used to love to explore, climbing rocks together in the sun, feeling like fellow lizards out there in the wild. You take the writer on one of your favorite secret slick-rock hikes, which leads to a waterfall that gushes into a deep pool. You explore the canyon beyond the trail, find a real Indian cave with petroglyphs, and when you come back to the waterfall, hot and parched from the dry desert sun, he suggests you jump in together. You are high up, a scary height, but he says you have to go for it, it's deep enough down below. You hold hands and jump off the cliff together, splashing into the cold pool, exhilarated. But when you get out, he's annoyed. He tells you he hadn't really been ready when you took the plunge.

You return to San Francisco and cook dinner for him one night. Over roast chicken he tells you he loves you. "That's sweet," you say, because something keeps you from telling him you love him, too.

After that, you don't hear from him. He doesn't call, he doesn't e-mail, and he won't answer his phone or even his doorbell. He simply disappears. You call a friend of his to determine that he's okay, he isn't in traction in a hospital somewhere, and the friend's wife says he's just acting like his usual self, wigging out, no surprise. Three weeks later, the writer finally calls, cheerful as yesterday, to see if he can drop by. He comes over and apologizes for his absence, saying he just wasn't ready for a relationship, he had to pull the emergency brake. He didn't want to meet your parents when they were in town. He just doesn't love you. Would you still play music with him? Go roller-blading? Then he has to leave, because, he explains, he has to meet up with another woman who lives across the Bay. He has to apologize to her, too. It's his day, he says, for making amends.

You are upset and disappointed. Right when you thought you

might be ready for a light relationship, you've carelessly opened your heart a crack just to allow some jerk to slam it shut.

The phone rings one evening soon after. It's the professor, who never calls. You didn't realize how much you needed to hear his deep, saucy voice. "I just wanted to say hello from across the Atlantic," he says. "I was thinking about you."

You tell him how happy you are to hear him, and when he asks what's up, you sigh. "The man I was seeing told me he loved me, and then he disappeared."

The professor makes a regretful clicking sound with his tongue. *"Poverina,"* he says. "Men can be so terrible."

It doesn't take long to get over the writer. You have experience getting over heartbreaks now, and this is just a minor chip. Mainly you are relieved that you didn't spend any more time with him. But you have a relapse when you go to Paris on a quick reporting trip. The professor is out of town, since no real Parisian is in town in August, which is fine: you don't want to enter into his world. You go to his Metro stop, to go look at his house, but even that feels too intrusive. You are part of his secret life, and you have no business there in the square where his kids play soccer. You get back on the next train.

You spend the evening at a small Italian restaurant, the one Marcello Mastroianni used to frequent when he was living in Paris, with a friend you know from San Francisco. You drink too much red wine and talk about past loves, and end up walking along the Seine, leaning over the stone bridge and watching the water below. It is a completely romantic spot, the moon reflected in the water flowing under the bridge, and so you talk about romance. "The thing is," he says, "when you get past the age of having children, then it doesn't make any sense to expect that any one relationship can be the center of your life. Different people give you different things you need. It's asking too much to have one relationship be everything. It's a setup for disappointment."

You nod along groggily. You aren't quite ready to join the past-the-age-of-having-children club, but you know what he means. You kiss cheeks good night, and you go back to your charming blue-and-buttercup hotel in the Marais. A little tipsy and weepy, you pick up the phone and dial the writer.

It's the middle of the day in San Francisco and he has a deadline, he needs to make money, he needs to work on his novel, he doesn't want to be disturbed.

"Listen," you say. "All I want to know is why the story had to end that way. Why couldn't we have just talked about it?" It was the same as with your husband: maybe the story had to end, but it didn't have to end so brutally, with so much disrespect. "When you get to a certain age, you can't expect one relationship to be the center of your life," you tell him. "We could have stayed friends. We didn't have to have such an ugly ending. Why couldn't we have talked about it?"

"We talked," he says crisply. "We're talking now. My lips are moving."

"You're the one," you say, "who told me you loved me."

"What's that?" he asks. "A social contract?"

"In some cultures it means something." You wipe your eyes.

"Where are you calling from?"

"Paris."

He pauses. "I can't believe," he finally says, "that you're using your trip to Paris to do this to me."

You don't know what he means. Then it occurs to you that one of his stories, a love story, takes place in Paris, and he must think you are calling from Paris to make some special point about him and relationships. Maybe he imagines you flew there just for that reason, to call him from there.

"Paris has nothing to do with it," you say. "I happen to be here, I had a few drinks, and I just don't understand why we had to have such a bad ending. We had fun together. I don't know why you had to hurt me like that. I can't *believe* you knew that I'd been abandoned by my husband so recently, you knew how much that hurt me, and then you just went ahead and did the same thing. Abandoned me."

"I'm supposed to take all of that into consideration?" asks the writer peevishly.

Suddenly you are completely sober. Your head has cleared. It's obvious that this man doesn't care about you, that he's incapable of caring about anyone but himself. Why are you wasting several dollars a minute on this cretin?

"Fuck you," you tell him. "Fuck you forever." And you hang up. It isn't a good ending, but it's a definite one.

By the end of the summer, the professor writes suggesting you go to the Aeolian Islands, the archipelago just north of mainland Sicily. You've always looked at those islands on the map, floating above Sicily, and dreamed about being there. You agree to meet in Naples.

You are still nervous about being in Naples by yourself, so you make a reservation at a nicer hotel than usual. You take a cab from the airport instead of a bus. The taxi driver is garrulous, pointing out all the sights along the way. You respond with enthusiasm, telling him you can't believe how beautiful the city is, in its distressed pastels and peeling ochers, perched right over the Mediterranean. He glances at you in the rearview mirror.

"Where did you learn Italian?" he asks, accelerating into a curve above the ocean. "You speak a beautiful, pure Italian."

"Grazie," you say. "In Florence, and in school."

"Toscana. Of course." That Tuscany is the fount of the purest Italian language is one of the few things Italians all over the country agree on. *"È bellissima,"* he says. You're amused at how he's figured out exactly how to get the best possible tip from you.

"Well," you say, "it is lovely to hear Napoletano spoken."

"Of course," he says, as if it were obvious, but pleased nonetheless. "Napoletano is the most beautiful dialect."

You arrive at your hotel, nap, and then take off to explore the city, since the professor isn't arriving until the next day. You have a map of the historic center, and wander through the streets, staring at one thirteenth-century or Renaissance church after another. Each corner, each building, is steeped in stories: here is San Lorenzo Maggiore, the church where Boccaccio first met Fiammetta in 1334, and where Petrarch took refuge during a tidal wave a few years later. Here is the Basilica di San Domenico Maggiore, where Saint Thomas Aquinas lived next door, and where a Caravaggio and a Titian are on display. There is the Duomo, where, mysteriously, flasks of Saint Gennaro's blood liquify every May and September. There is Piazza Bellini, with street-side cafés, where you can see the remains of the ancient Greek city walls. In the alleys, children play soccer, dodging the laundry lines, and adults playing cards outside their front doors. Whole families of four zip by on single *motorinos.* Elderly women bathe in the water by the port and sun themselves on the rocks, with Vesuvius and Ischia in their sights. Naples, far from being a seedy, dangerous city, has untold layers of charm, a faded beauty who can still wield her seductive wiles.

As dusk comes, you walk along the park that borders the bay. It is a Saturday night, and everyone is out strolling in pairs or groups. The weather is sultry, and the young men and women in love are unabashed, the men sitting backwards against the handlebars of their parked *motorinos,* the women straddling the bikes, facing the men, kissing and caressing away. No one even glances at them. Better, it seems, to make out passionately in public than to go altogether too far in private.

You are almost the only person out walking alone. When you get tired of the people-watching, the rickety carousels, the stands selling coconut slices and corn on the cob, the groups of teenagers on *motorinos,* you look for a place to eat. You find a little pizzeria on a side street, and sit at a table outside. The waiter, who looks like Al Pacino, gives you special attention since you're eating alone. He brings you a glass of fizzy young white wine, a salad, and a pizza napoletana, with fresh mozzarella, intensely flavorful tomatoes, fresh anchovies and a thin golden brown crust. Afterward, you tell him that although there's pizza everywhere in the United States, *dappertutto,* you've never in your life tasted real pizza before today. He loves hearing that, and brings you a perfect espresso, with creamy foam on top in the shape of a heart.

The next day you wake up too late, jet-lagged, to go to the archaeological museum, with all its treasures from Pompeii and Herculaneum. It's just as well, because now you know you'll have to return to Naples one day. It's Sunday, everything is closed, so you wander the streets again, taking a tram up to the top of a hill, walking around in the sun, listening to people having loud arguments from their balconies, admiring the exquisite produce for sale at every corner grocery. You drift back down to the grand Piazza del Plebiscito, a huge plaza half circled with columns, and watch a bride and groom on a motorcycle, the bride's voluminous white train trailing in the street behind her, a beautiful couple, completely joyful.

You wait for the professor on the terrace of the hotel. You're nervous; you never quite believe that you will actually see each other again, or that your transcontinental plans won't go awry. He finally arrives, hours late, looking much more like himself than he had in London. He's shed his overcoat for a thin denim jacket and his curls are touched with sun. You hug each other, relieved; it's at once so comfortable and so strange to hold each other again after seven months. He sits with you on your chaise longue, stroking your summer dress, looking at the view over the bay. "You always manage to find a beautiful spot," he says.

He looks at his watch. You have to leave in order to make your boat in good time, but first, you have to shop for a picnic. The professor always brings a picnic to eat on board a boat. You go from one shop to another to find the best prosciutto, grapes, bread, olives, and wine. You board the boat and eat dinner on the deck, watching the lights of Naples shimmer on the bay. When the boat finally pulls out, it is dark.

You go below deck to your cramped cabin, claustrophobic at first, where you manage to snuggle together on one of the thin bunk beds, the boat eventually rocking you toward sleepiness. The professor climbs up to his bunk and turns the lights out. In what seems like only a few minutes, he's up again, bumping around the dark.

"What is it?" you ask.

"Le stelle," he says. "You have to get up and see the stars."

"Now?"

"You can sleep, *principessa,* but I'm going out. It's almost dawn."

You slip on your dress and the Egyptian scarf he gave you and follow him out. The professor is up near the bow. No one else is awake, and a few young travelers are huddled in bags on the deck, sleeping. The stars are brilliant, crowded in the black sky. The professor stands behind you, and wraps his arms around your waist, warming you both. "Beautiful stars," you say. "So many."

"Watch over there," he says, pointing in the distance. "Don't take your eyes off it."

You stare at the darkness, with no idea what he's talking about. Suddenly, a flaming torch of orange appears on the horizon. Astonishing.

"Stromboli," says the professor.

"A volcano? Erupting?"

"Sì."

You watch the sky, and every fifteen or twenty minutes the volcano erupts, closer and closer, until you can make out a red shower of cinders spewing from the glow. The sky grows lighter as you approach Stromboli, it is dawn, and by the time you pull into the harbor, you can no longer see the crater. You can't believe people actually live on an island with a live volcano.

"I climbed the volcano fifteen years ago," says the professor, transported. "I camped up there and watched the volcano erupt during the night."

"Wasn't that dangerous?"

"Not if you didn't get too close. But the sound was frightening. It made a huge, thundering noise."

"Do you want to do it again?" You're excited.

"No, no," says the professor. "It would be too changed for me, just as the Sinai was for you. But you should. You absolutely must climb the volcano."

The ship pulls out of the main port of Stromboli, takes on some passengers in a rowboat from the small town of Ginostra on the other side, then heads to Panarea, the flashiest of the seven Aeolian islands, where the best-dressed passengers disembark. You change boats at graceful, twin-hilled Salina, and then, passing the largest island of Lipari, finally land at one of the outermost islands.

The island is rocky and somewhat bleak, with dry vegetation and only a few ragged buildings near the port: a restaurant, a hotel, and one or two grocery stores. The island, a dormant volcano, rises steeply from the little town and its surrounding jagged rocks to high, terraced hills, where white houses cling to the sides. A van from your hotel picks you up, and the woman driving gives you an orientation to the island in about two minutes. The island has been inhabited, on and off, since prehistoric times, and now there are about four hundred souls living here—fishing, gathering capers, servicing the few tourists who manage to find themselves in the far reaches of the archipelago. The rock terraces, she says, have been there since before the time of the Romans, stones piled on top of stones for centuries.

At the hotel, the signora takes your passports, making a slightly disapproving face at the odd pair, the burgundy French one and the blue American one. She shows you to your room, which has a great view of the ocean, but which opens right out onto the restaurant. The professor refuses it—*impossibile!*—but the signora says there is no other. Finally, after you make it clear you don't want the room, even if you have to take a boat to another island, she finds a nearby house, with a terrace, for the same price. "Perfect," says the professor. He takes up residence in the hammock and smokes a cigar, looking out across the white stucco walls and bougainvillea to the volcanic islands dotting the sea in the distance.

In the afternoon, you walk all the way down to the rocky beach, about two miles. You situate yourselves on some of the slippery black boulders, trying to get comfortable. The professor lies back, delighted, listening to the waves, feeling the sun on his face. You put on sunblock, a hat, a long-sleeved shirt, and lean against a rock. You've come to a place where there are no distractions; there is absolutely nothing to do but sit on the beach, eat, and make love. It's lovely, but the expanse of ten days makes you wonder if, with no museums or city sights to entertain you, you'll get tired of being alone with each other.

"Maybe," you venture, "we could hire one of those boats and go explore the grotto on the other side of the island."

"You go right ahead," the professor says. "I'm not doing anything like that."

You open your book.

About an hour later, the professor shifts his body to even out his tan. "You know," he says, "my wife could never tolerate this, ten days of doing nothing on a beach. She's so energetic, she always has to be doing something dynamic. Even if she's at the beach, she wants it to be one with lots of waves, lots of action." He says that admiringly.

You know what his wife meant. "It's nice that you never say

anything negative about your wife," you tell him. The little he has spoken of her has always been with enormous respect for her taste, her intelligence, and her good sense. It's plain, in fact, how much the professor adores his wife—even if it seems that something, and he would never divulge what, is somehow sad between them.

"In many ways," he says, "we have an exceptional relationship."

You sit in the sun and go out for long swims. "You know, professor," you say, returning to your spot, "I'm not sure I know what I'll do here for ten days, either. It's a challenge to relax."

"You write articles, you write books, you travel by yourself, and you think *this* is a challenge?" asks the professor.

"Well, yes," you say.

"You have to get into the rhythm, the rhythm of *far niente,* doing nothing. It's good for you."

You settle back with your book.

"What did you bring this time?" asks the professor. By now he knows your mania for bringing books that are set in the place you're visiting. It was hard to find one about the Aeolian Islands.

"The Odyssey."

"Homer's *Odyssey?"*

Odysseus, you say, had gone to one of the Aeolian islands on his journey home from Troy. The island was the home of Aeolus, the god of the winds. You read to the professor from the Robert Fagles translation. "A great floating island it was, and round it all huge ramparts rise of indestructible bronze and sheer rock cliffs shoot up from sea to sky." You do your best to translate it into Italian for him.

The professor stares up at the cliffs above you. "Nothing has changed," he says. "The simple and ancient things, the things that give you the most pleasure, never change. This view has hardly ever changed. The sea is always the sea, the night is the night, and the stars, the stars."

"Don't forget the fish, the olive oil, and the wine," you say.

"Giusto," says the professor. "And the sex. Sex is so ancient and simple." He puts his hands behind his head and closes his eyes. Then he opens them again. "So what happened to Odysseus on the island? A bag of wind or something?"

"Right." Aeolus had given Odysseus a bag of wind and sped him along his way. But when Odysseus's crew opened the bag to see what plunder it contained, the winds swept them all the way back to the Aeolians—where Aeolus refused to help the cursed Odysseus again.

"If I were Odysseus," says the professor, contemplating the rocky coast, "I never would have left Calypso, the nymph. She made love to him all day and promised him immortality if he would be her boyfriend forever."

"But he didn't love her," you say. "He had to return to his true wife, Penelope."

The professor lights a cigarette and smokes quietly for a few moments, contemplating the pale rings against the blue sky. "Well, yes," he says. "*He* had someone to return to who loved him."

The professor, you can only suppose, does not. Even though you can't imagine his life in Paris, you realize your escapes probably mean as much to him as they do to you.

The next morning, the professor, mindful that you are nervous about getting bored on the island, pulls out a miniature chess set. You tell him that you haven't played in years, and that the last time you tried, your boyfriend beat you twelve times in a row before you gave up. You hate feeling stupid, and you've always felt one step behind the professor, intellectually—he speaks Italian better, he knows so much more about all the art you see, he grazes through philosophy books as if they were summer novels. Chess?

"No way," you say.

"It'll be fun," he promises. He starts arranging the pieces on the wooden table on the whitewashed terrace. He has to remind you which way the pieces move.

You play a plodding game at first, you mimicking his moves, he eating a few of your pawns. Then you come up with a plan to sacrifice one of your knights, play stupid, and then make a sneak attack from behind. He falls for it, picking off your knight with relish.

"Una strage!" you exclaim, a massacre, using one of those odd words you learned in your Italian fable class.

Your strategy plays out perfectly, and before long you have him in checkmate. The professor is a little flustered. "Sometimes," he says, "even my son can beat me at first."

You shrug. "I was just lucky," you agree. Then you start rearranging the pieces. "Wanna play again?"

All that sitting around reading and playing chess has given you an enormous appetite. You make your way down the long, steep path to the port, where you have lunch at the restaurant that overlooks the harbor. It seems exceptionally lucky that a tiny island with only a couple of restaurants has such wonderful food—fresh grilled fish, *caponata,* cherry tomato salad with capers. All with a warm breeze drifting through the outdoor terrace, all with a view of volcanic islands in the distance. You start with grilled eggplant rolled around fresh ricotta, jump over the pasta course, as the professor puts it, then polish off a huge plate of fresh octopus, shrimp, and fish, all with a half liter of young white wine.

You spend four days in a languorous rhythm. You wake up in the morning, make espresso, and sit quietly, watching the morning boats go in and out of the harbor, leaving trails behind them like snails. Then you go back to bed and make love, dreamily, until it's hard to know whether you should get up or go back to sleep. You read or play another increasingly intense game of chess (the professor makes a strenuous comeback, insisting you finally stop when you are even, four to four). Then you pack your beach bags, and decide which of the two restaurants you want to eat at—the nearby rose-colored restaurant, or the one at the port. You have a long espresso and then make your way to the beach.

"I love that you know the water is warm enough that you aren't shocked when you get in, you can't even feel a change in temperature," says the professor, taking off his shorts. "All this time, and I haven't worn my swimsuit once." He floats out into the water.

"*Delizioso,*" he says. "There's no other word."

"What day is today?" you ask him, rubbing sunscreen on your legs.

"I don't know," he says. "Tuesday?"

"I mean the date." He counts up from the day you left. "September ninth," he says.

"Today would have been my fourth wedding anniversary," you say. Four years since that day when your husband married you, an ecstatic grin on his face, under the grove of redwood trees. Four years is as long as college. You're a different person now.

The professor paddles around, climbs out of the water, and reaches for his towel. "You know what makes me happy?" he asks.

"What, professor?"

"You never mention your ex-husband's name. You hardly ever talk about him at all anymore."

"I guess I must have talked about him too much before," you say.

"That's natural."

"I really don't think about him much anymore," you say. To your surprise, that's true.

"Do you ever see him?"

You tell him you ran into him on the street in San Francisco one day. It was perfect timing: a friend had just treated you to lunch at one of your favorite restaurants, where you had oysters and Sauvignon Blanc, an arugula salad, split a wood-fired pizza, and finished it all up with espresso and a grappa. You were feeling no pain. You ran into your husband, and he greeted you, looking the same as ever in his blue fleece jacket and lightweight hiking shoes, on his way to a board meeting where everyone else would probably be wearing suits. You were surprised to find that your anger had disappeared, that you were thinking he really wasn't such a bad guy, he just hadn't been right for you. Before you knew what you were doing, you gave him a big hug. He pulled away and asked you how you were. You said you were doing just fine.

"Do you want to talk sometime?" Jon asked. "You can always call me."

"No," you told him. "It's nice to run into you, but I really don't have anything else to say."

"*Giusto,*" says the professor. "That story is closed."

After four or five days, you're running out of money (not every remote island in the world has an ATM machine) and decide to go to the island of Lipari, where there are some banks and shops. The professor has no interest in getting up from his hammock, and requests only that you bring him back some filterless cigarettes. *"Povera Laura,"* he says, from the hammock. "Poor girl has to leave this paradise to go deal with civilization."

"Anything besides the cigarettes, professor?"

"Everything else, we have right here," he says, gesturing around him. He looks at his watch. "If I were you, I would get going," he says, not making a move.

You hike down to the port, take the boat to Lipari, the largest of the islands, whose sides are grated away by pumice mining, and where the beaches are long and white. You climb up from the port to the castle, with its thick stone walls built to fend off Turkish pirates in the sixteenth century. There is an archaeological museum here, and you dutifully trek through room after room of pottery shards, marveling at how anyone could ever date a pottery shard, and why. You finally work your way up to Etruscan pots and stacks of amphorae that were discovered from ships that sank off Filicudi island's rocky shoals. The long trip through the museum buildings has a big payoff: In the last building is a collection of almost a thousand fourth century A.D. terra-cotta Greek theater masks and figurines. There are characters from the plays of Sophocles, Euripedes, Aristophanes, and Dionysian figures dancing, drinking, and shaking tambourines; there are innumerable human archetypes—the worried man, the chatterbox, the laughing old woman, the conniving youth, all with wonderfully expressive faces. And there is Aeolus himself, puffing his big cheeks out to blow a burst of wind.

You have lunch at a pizzeria, walk around the shops, consider the odds of a set of red ceramic plates painted with caper berries making it back unshattered to San Francisco, find some filterless cigarettes, buy some malvasia from a signora who tells you at great length how she made it, and just make the hydrofoil back to your island. The boat is late, and there's no professor to meet you. You hike back up the long, stair-stepped trail built into the steep hill, back to your little house, but he isn't there, either. You open the bottle of malvasia, the sweet white fortified wine that Odysseus's men drank by the amphora, and have a glass. Finally, the professor returns, worn out. He's had a long day; he hiked all over the island, tried to meet your boat, and ended up having a drink with a woman who said she recognized him from a tent they'd shared in Yugoslavia a few years ago.

"Did you really share a tent with her?"

"I was in Yugoslavia in a tent with a woman, but probably before she was born," he says, chuckling to himself over the incident.

"And so?" you ask.

"So, it was entertaining."

"And would you have wanted to be in a tent in Yugoslavia with her?"

"Come no," he says. Why not. "She was cute." Then he catches himself. "But not as cute as you, *cara.*"

You leave him alone for one day, you think, and he finds another woman, even on a desolate island with only a few hundred inhabitants. His poor wife.

You eat dinner at the nearby restaurant, drink some malvasia on your terrace, and make love. "My dear," he says to you, when you are lying back, spent. "You have no idea what you do to me. If you had any idea at all, you would be impossible."

"Okay, okay," you say. "You can go back to dreaming about your tent."

That evening it storms, with lightning illuminating the broad sky. The seas are furious, historically the roughest in the Mediterranean, and if there had been a ship trying to seek shelter along Capo Graziano, the rocky edge of Filicudi, it could well have sunk like so many had before.

It storms again in the morning, and then it's cloudy, and you don't get down to the beach until the sun finally peeks out in the afternoon. The professor takes a swim in the nude, and suggests it's so refreshing you do the same. There are no boats around, so you swim out. When you return, the professor complains. "I don't like it when you swim so far," he says. "It's dangerous."

"It's okay," you tell him. "It's calm, there are no currents, no sea lions, and I'm strong."

"Stay closer," he insists.

You go out a second time, and get stung by a jellyfish on your chest. You are starting to feel like prey: little no-see-um flies have eaten you up during the night, you are covered with bites, and now a jellyfish has stung you. The professor makes sympathetic noises without looking up from his philosophy book. You sit in the sun trying to soothe the bite, rubbing your chest where the jellyfish had stung you.

"This island," you tell the professor, trying to get comfortable on the rocks, "isn't an easy place to be. It's beautiful, but . . ."

"It isn't easy," he agrees. "But it's a pleasure, not a comfort.

They're different. A pleasure you remember long after you forget about whether you were comfortable or covered in little bites."

Easy for him to say. You need to cool your sting in the water. You swim out again, exploring a nearby cove, and come back in, hauling yourself up on the slippery rocks. You place your hand on a round rock in the water and feel a dog bite on your little finger. You snatch it away and it is badly grated, staining the water. You come back to the professor, holding up your finger.

"It's bleeding," you say.

The professor stares at the blood flowing from your finger. "It's a beautiful color," he says. "You would never believe that color of blood in a movie, but it's beautiful."

"It's blood!" you say. Now is not the time to be so fucking aesthetic. "I'm bleeding!"

"Okay, okay," he says. *"Tranquilla."* He studies your finger.

"It's *really* bleeding," he concludes. He wraps it up in his handkerchief, with a rubber band. He helps you back into your clothes, dressing you like a child, and holds you carefully while you walk back to the road. The hanky is already sodden with blood.

He finds a hotel van that is taking guests up to the top of the hill, near your little house, and asks them to take you. There's no room for him in the van, so he reluctantly leaves, saying he'll buy dinner and meet you later.

You greet the hotel driver, show him your reddened hanky, and tell him you've been bitten by something.

"La murena," he murmurs knowingly, glancing to see if the tourists in the van understand. "You'd better see the doctor." He drops off the hotel guests and takes you straight to the doctor's office, a little building near the rose-colored restaurant on the

hill. A plastic chair at the entrance to the room has several cardboard signs, each scrawled with the name and telephone number of a different bar or restaurant where the doctor can be found. The driver telephones the number on the sign that's up in the window today, and the doctor, a thin grave man, arrives a few minutes later.

"*La murena,*" the hotel driver explains to the doctor.

The doctor dismisses that with a wave of his hand. "*Impossibile,*" he says. He looks at you. "You must have scratched this on the rock. You hardly ever see *la murena* around here. If it was *la murena,* you wouldn't have a finger left."

"Someone ate me!" you say, losing some Italian with all that blood.

"It was la *murena!*" the hotel driver argues.

"Rocks!"

"*Murena!*"

"Rocks!"

"*Murena!*" Everyone is gesturing wildly.

"*Murena!*" you say, flinging your pinkie finger out in all the excitement, then holding it again gingerly. You hadn't actually seen the moray eel, but something had definitely bitten you. Plus, it makes a better story, especially if everyone usually loses a finger. You're hoping for a big scar.

The doctor unwraps your pinkie, which is mangled on the tip, with a big gash. He squirts antiseptic on it and peers at it.

"*Murena,*" he finally concedes. He explains how moray eels have prehensile jaws that once clamped down don't open again. That's why you'd had to tear your finger out. "You should have lost your finger," he says, as if you'd done something wrong.

The hotel driver grins, victorious, and the doctor impatiently waves him out of the examining room. He examines your pinkie.

"Ironing?" you ask him.

He presses his fingers together, what the hell did you mean, ironing?

You make stitching motions and he gets it. Sewing.

"No stitches," he says. "No need to exaggerate." The doctor wraps up your finger with a lot of gauze, and then asks you where you are from, and who you are traveling with. You tell him, and change the gender of your friend. It always seems a little *puttanesco* to be unmarried, but no longer young, and traveling with a male friend in that part of the world. The doctor is surprised, and mildly offended, that you offer payment for his services, which strikes you as a rather civilized way for a country to handle health care. While you are at it, you ask him if he has anything to calm down all the millions of no-see-um bites you have. You show him how your arms and legs are covered with bites. He nods and pulls out a syringe. You roll up your sleeve. He shakes his head no. You understand and lean over the table. The one time you have to go to a doctor in an emergency, and not only aren't you wearing nice, clean underwear, you aren't wearing any underwear at all.

Embarrassed, you thank him, and walk back to the house, where the professor has arranged a picnic dinner. He ascertains that you are fine, and teases you that at least the moray eel that bit you was certainly going to die of poisoning. As you watch the sun go down, it begins to storm, with lightning that makes Salina appear and disappear in ghostly flashes. The thunder grows louder and longer and closer. The rain pounds on the terrace. *"Un temporale,"* the professor breathes. *"Una tempesta."* It is beautiful to watch, and you are happy to be snug in your house, not out on a boat at sea. Then the electricity on the entire island goes out. You find a candle and have dinner, watching the sky, the house shuddering with the winds, and then make your way to bed as the rain bangs against the door. You hold each other tight, a little scared.

"A dramatic day," says the professor.

"Still a pleasure," you say, and fall asleep.

The next day, unbelievably, is your last on the island. Your plane leaves in three days, but you want to spend a day on Stromboli to climb the volcano. The professor refuses to go back to Stromboli in this lifetime, so you decide that the next day you will go there yourself, and then meet up with the professor on the boat back to Naples, which stops at Stromboli, the day after that.

You go to have dinner at the rose-colored restaurant on your last night. The professor tidies up his things and leaves the room. You close the door and follow him. He goes back in for cigarettes.

"You left the light on," he says. Then he surveys the room. The drawers with your stuff are open, and a few of your things are strewn around. "You are always leaving everything open," he nitpicks. He plucks a wet swimsuit that you had left on the bed and hands it to you.

"I'm sorry," you retort, throwing it over the clothesline on the terrace. "I'm on vacation."

He starts walking toward the restaurant.

"Wait," you say. "How cold do you think it is? Do you think a scarf is okay? Or do I need a sweater, too?"

"I don't know," he says, annoyed. "You decide."

"Just a scarf, then," you say.

"*Va bene,*" he says.

You walk out to the road. "Wait," you say. "I think I need a sweater."

The professor is exasperated. "You catch up with me," he says, and keeps on walking. "And close everything."

By the time you reach the restaurant, he has found a table. The young waiter with slicked-back hair comes up and apologizes that they are not serving *la murena* that night; everyone, it seems, has heard the story of the Americana getting bitten. He whips out his pad and pen and asks you what number you'd like to pick for your table. He's writing the numbers on the paper tablecloths to keep track.

"Non so," says the professor. I don't know.

"Well, why don't you pick the date you were married?" the waiter asks.

"La brutta verità," says the professor, the ugly truth is that you aren't married.

The waiter nods knowingly, and writes a number. You aren't sure the professor needed to embarrass you that way.

"Why can't you just give him a number instead of telling him we're not married?" you ask him.

"Who cares?" says the professor.

"It just calls attention to our situation," you say.

"They don't care," says the professor.

"I care," you say. "I don't like to feel like I'm having an affair with someone. I want to feel like I belong."

"Okay, okay," he says. You quietly study the menus for a while, even though you know them by heart after four days. When the waiter reappears, the professor orders a bottle of good wine, your last dinner together. You also order your two favorite pasta dishes on the menu, which might actually be the two best pastas in the world. He has *maccheroncini alla Norma,* with ripe tomatoes, eggplant, onion, oil, basil, and fresh ricotta salata. You order an amazingly savory *pasta con le sarde.*

When the dishes come, you compliment the signora on the pasta, and finally get up the nerve to ask her how it's made. She seems surprised, as if everyone in the world knows how to make *pasta con le sarde,* and indeed, everyone in her world probably does. But she humors you, patiently describing the dish. First you make a *soffritto,* sautéing finely chopped onion and anchovies in olive oil, dissolving the anchovies, then you toss in some fresh sardines (heads and tails cut off). Meanwhile, you boil some salted water, parboil the fennel, and then reserve the water and smash the fennel (the translation is a little rough). Add the fennel to the sardine mixture, and cook for ten minutes or so. Then you add a few sultanas and pine nuts, as well as a smidge of saffron. You cook some bucatini in the boiling fennel water, *al dente,* then you mix it, energetically, into the sardine mixture—the strong-armed signora makes a mixing motion—and let it rest a few minutes before serving.

The professor and you are transported by the pasta, by the courtyard with potted plants, tiles, and old metal boat parts hung on the walls. You are back in a good mood.

"It's gone by so fast," you say. "It's been such a short time together."

"You were worried about being bored with all this time on a remote island."

"I adjusted. If the fall weren't definitely setting in, I think I would stay longer."

"It would be possible," says the professor, "to stay here forever."

You take a sip of wine. *"Mi sento bene con te,"* you tell him. I feel good with you.

"You are perfect for vacation," he says. "I don't think I could live with you, but you are perfect for vacation."

You put down your glass. You know what the professor is saying is true, and he's teasing, but you don't want to hear it. Part of you fantasizes that if he wasn't married, you might learn French, move to Paris, and cook *pasta con le sarde* for him every Sunday. You could buy a little house on one of these islands, install a hammock here and retire later on. You don't think you would ever get tired of the professor. "Right," you say.

"And what if I lived in San Francisco?" asks the professor. *"Troppo complicato?"* Too complicated?

"If you lived in San Francisco, you wouldn't be you," you say. You take another sip of wine. Your eyes are starting to tear, and you are mad at yourself about it.

"What is it, *cara*?" asks the professor, putting a hand on your forearm.

"Nothing," you say.

"Dai," says the professor. "What?"

"I just—" you wipe your eyes. "I just don't like hearing that I'm only good for vacation. I mean that's the situation, and I love being on vacation with you, but I don't like feeling that I'm just a woman who is only good for being on vacation, not for having a real relationship."

The professor sighs. "I didn't say that, Laura. I'm sure there are many men who would love to live with you, who would be lucky to have you. You're witty, you're warm—"

You cut him off. You want *him* to want you, to wish that you could be together, even if you couldn't. You can't help it. You're going to cry again.

"Don't," says the professor. "Don't."

You excuse yourself to the restroom, splash water on your face, and return to the table, more composed.

The professor is smoking a cigarette. He exhales the smoke from the side of his mouth. "You know," he says, "it might be better for you if you traveled in Italy without me."

"Why?" you say. Would he rather not be with you? You're in danger of crying again.

"I get in your way," he says. "A woman like you, who speaks Italian, blonde, could meet a lot of Italian men. You need to meet men you might have a relationship with, and that's impossible when you're with me."

"But I like being with you," you say.

"I like being with you, too, *cara,*" he says. He looks at you directly with his watery blue eyes. "But I don't matter. It would be better for you."

You make a gesture brushing away what he is saying. "No, no," you say. "You are perfect for vacation."

In the morning, you pack your things quietly. He puts on his frayed denim shirt that has a tear in the sleeve. "*È morta,*" he says. It's dead. He decides to leave it behind instead of packing it.

"I'll take it," you say. You put on his soft shirt, take some photos of the professor in the hammock, having a cigarette after his coffee, and of the two of you together on the terrace. The driver from the hotel arrives to take your things down to the port. The professor turns to you and gives you a big hug before you go down the steps to the car. "It's been great," he says, in English. "You are such a sweet girl."

"*Grazie,*" you say, kissing him on both cheeks.

You buy your tickets and board the *aliscafo* for Salina. You stand on the stern of the boat and wave good-bye to an island you will probably never return to, at least not with the professor. As you head for Salina, where the professor is going to spend the day, and you are switching boats, he tells you that his boat to Naples will pull in to Stromboli at nine the next evening. If you want to return with him, you can catch the boat then. If not, if you want to spend more time in Italy, you can come to wave good-bye.

"It might be better for you," he says, "to stay on for a few days. You might meet a nice Italian man."

You throw your scarf over your shoulder and give him a wink. "Maybe I will," you say playfully, though you think the chances are pretty slim.

When the boat stops at Salina, where he is getting off to visit a friend, and you are making a connection to Stromboli, he gives you a quick kiss. "See you," he says.

"Maybe soon," you say. Maybe not, you think, uneasily. You disembark like strangers. He walks straight into the little port town without looking back. He has such a loose, languid way of moving, completely at home in the Mediterranean. In the distance, he spots the friend he is visiting on the island and greets him. They don't shake hands or grasp shoulders, the way American male friends do. They kiss each other, three times, and then walk off, touching arms.

NINE

STROMBOLI

The professor disappears. You immediately miss his comforting presence, but are excited to be traveling by yourself again. Anything could happen. You don't know whether you will meet up with him the next evening when his boat to Naples stops off in Stromboli, or maybe stay for a few more days in the islands, as he'd suggested. You wonder whether he'd be disappointed—or even relieved—if you did stay longer.

You study the people sitting on the white wooden benches across from you, who are also waiting for the next boat to Stromboli. There are a couple of scruffy French-speaking kids with woven bracelets and backpacks who are talking to two Italian men in their thirties. One of the Italians is tall and golden tan, with the wind blowing his faded turquoise T-shirt against his stomach. He's wearing a goofy, beat-up Panama hat, but his face seems serious, curious, as if he's taking everything in. He senses you staring at him, and you quickly return to your book. The other, a chubby, dark-haired, olive-skinned, true gesturing-as-he-speaks Italian, is describing what he knows about Stromboli in French to the young couple. You strain to understand what he is saying, because you have no idea what you are going to do when you get off on Stromboli, either. So far your only plan is to climb the volcano, and that's sketchy. You don't even have a guidebook. The dark-haired Italian looks you up and down, and whispers something to his buddy in the turquoise T-shirt. You turn away. The *aliscafo* arrives and you all hoist your bags aboard.

The boat pulls away, and the houses on the island shrink until they're square white pebbles on a faraway beach, with sparse green mountains rising behind them. Dark clouds bunch around the island peaks, but the sky is clear over the sea. You lean over the railing, feeling the sun and the mist on your face.

As Stromboli comes into view, a small dark triangle, you head to the bow to watch the volcano. Smoke rises from the cone in thick fingers, darker and dirtier than the surrounding clouds. The small bow is crowded, so you sit on some narrow metal steps that lead up to the captain's perch.

"*Scusi, signorina.*" You look up and see the Italian with the Panama hat. He is being a little flip, since a southern Italian man who is a total stranger won't usually call a woman who is over thirty *signorina,* out of respect. He asks if you mind if he sits down since there is nowhere else to sit. You nod and he squeezes in next to you, his shoulder grazing yours. He smells like saltwater and soap. A few minutes go by, and then a burst of smoke rises and tumbles out of the volcano.

"That was a good one," he says. You give him a somewhat discouraging smile. He takes off his hat and runs his fingers through his toffee-colored ringlets. He has wire-rimmed glasses and sleepy blue eyes, big pillowy lips, and a strong, stubbly jaw. He gestures at the landscape in front of him. "I love islands," he says, then looks directly at you, giving you a little shiver. "Are *you* from an island?" You shake your head no, and pause.

"A peninsula, really," you say. "I do live near the ocean."

He tries to guess where you are from, winding his way from Australia and New Zealand to Denmark and England, finally landing in the United States, where he's never been. "I would have to learn English," he says. "Of course I should learn English, everyone should, but I haven't." Besides Italian, he's sorry to say, he speaks only a little French and Spanish.

"I'm not so sure everyone should learn English," you say. "Americans ought to make an effort to learn something else."

"It's not a pretty language," he says. "It has no music to it."

"It's not like Italian," you agree, "but English is a beautiful language, a remarkably precise language, with a million words to choose from to deliver your exact shade of meaning."

"That's what makes it so terrible to learn."

You tell him you are from California, and he wonders why in the world you have made your way to these remote, godforsaken little islands. You explain that you are traveling with a friend, the Italian word giving away the gender of the friend, and then he knows more about you than you want him to.

"Where is he?" he asks, raising an eyebrow. You explain that he stayed on another island, that you had wanted to come to Stromboli to climb the volcano. He cocks his head, puzzled: Americans might behave this way, but he can't fathom an Italian letting his woman leave to go climb a volcano by herself.

You ask him where he's from, and he asks if you know Taranto. When you say no, he shows you the inside of his left forearm, which is lean and strong. He points to a tender spot halfway between his elbow crease and wrist and makes an X. "Roma," he says. Then he points to his jutting outside wrist bone: "Napoli." His four long fingers are Basilicata and Calabria, and finally he wiggles his thumb. "Puglia," he says. "I am from the Greek hand of Italy."

You chat; he is a saxophone teacher at a music conservatory, teaching classical music. He asks if you play music, and you tell him jazz piano, badly.

"You have the hands for it," he observes. And he, you think, has the lips to play the saxophone.

You hold your hands out in front of you. "I guess I have long fingers," you say, *ditos*.

"Dita," he corrects you. "The plural is irregular."

You fold your arms. "Sorry," you say, "my Italian isn't so hot." You're sure the professor always says *"ditos."*

"No, no, *I'm* sorry," he says, touching you lightly on the arm. "Your Italian is quite good. I wouldn't have thought an American could speak so well. If it weren't so good, I never would have noticed a little mistake like that."

There are twenty-one verb tenses in Italian, and he had just used about half of them. "Thank you," you say.

"It's a rare pleasure to run into an American woman you can have a conversation with," he says. It's a rare pleasure to run into such a gorgeous man who seems so friendly. You haven't been noticing any Italian men at all, since you've been with the professor, and suddenly they are coming into focus.

He quizzes you at length about your piano lessons, how your teacher approaches theory, telling you how difficult it was for him to go back to thinking like a beginner. You talk about music you like, agreeing on all the jazz greats. He is a bit of a snob: when you tell him you like Pino Daniele—a compliment to a southern Italian, you figure—he says only the old stuff is any good, the recent albums are all commercial pop. And Andrea

Bocelli? Well, he says, it's romantic, but really, either you sing opera or you don't. You are a little defensive on that point—there's nothing better, you think, than turning up Andrea Bocelli really loud and making soup in the winter—but you let it rest.

When the hydrofoil slows down to a sputter, he offers you his hand, and introduces himself as Fabio. You slide your hand from his after a second too long and tell him your name. His dark-haired friend appears, and Fabio, very formally, says he would like to introduce his new friend Laura from San Francisco. Laura, Pasquale. *Piacere.* A pleasure to meet you. And you.

Pasquale scrutinizes you. "Laura," he says, "is an Italian name. You don't look very Italian."

You admit that, unfortunately, you don't have a single drop of Italian blood. But Laura, you inform him, is an American name, too. And that includes Latin America. The good thing about being named Laura, you tell him, is that it works just about anywhere. Unlike, for example, Pasquale.

Pasquale considers that. "Sorry," he says. "Laura is Italian."

The first Laura in literature, Fabio points out—Petrarch's Laura, in the 1300s—was Italian. He looks off into the distance as if he could conjure her up. "Laura, the mysterious, beautiful muse." Fabio is clearly a romantic.

"That Laura," you tell him, "was a figment of Petrarch's imagination." She existed, you say, but he had no idea who she really was; he'd seen her only from a distance. The one time they spoke, she told him he must be mistaking her for someone else. It was all in his head. *"Secondo me,"* you tell them, according to you—the phrase Italians use to preface and disarm any outrageous opinion—Petrarch was a narcissist, and his love for Laura was just a projection. How could he really have loved her? He didn't even know her.

"That," says Fabio, giving you a look, "must be the hazard of being a beautiful Laura."

"Yeah, right," you say in English. You love the way he says your name.

"I'm not calling an American woman 'Laura,' " Pasquale concludes, crossing his arms, "I'm calling her Molly." He pronounces it "moley," which is awful. He is delighted with himself, and looks to Fabio for agreement.

Fabio is thinking it over.

"Laura," you quickly interject, "also happens to be the name of a great jazz tune, one that saxophone players are particularly fond of. Charlie Parker recorded it, and so did Eric Dolphy."

Fabio spreads his arms wide, as if to embrace you. *"Laura!"* he says.

"Molly," says Pasquale, unmoved.

The *aliscafo* pulls into the harbor. Fabio, picking up your bag for you, mentions that since you are all in the same situation, they'll be happy to help you find a place to stay. You tell them thanks, but you can take care of yourself. You disembark, and they quickly locate a signora who is offering cheap rooms in a nearby *pensione*. They signal you to follow.

"Va bene?" asks Fabio. You say you'll see.

A skinny boy leads you up the narrow street from the port. Motor scooters whiz by, and you plaster yourselves against the whitewashed buildings to make room for the three-wheeled scooter trucks. Compared with the island you've been on, Stromboli seems like a metropolis. You turn into an alley, and the boy slides a skeleton key into an ancient flaking blue door. Inside is a dim passageway with a tiny kitchen and a dark bedroom off to the side, with rickety cots, sheets on the windows, and pastel

prints of saints tacked up on the walls. You are considering parting company with these guys, fast. Then the boy leads you up a
flight of stairs to a concrete terrace with plastic chairs, and up
another flight to a locked room on top with a little balcony.
Everything changes: from here, you have a view of the island
that spreads out to the sea, with Strombolicchio, the rugged
rock promontory offshore, in view.

"You can't have that island over there," Fabio calls from
the terrace below, gesturing to Strombolicchio, "it's mine."

You look down at him, and he looks back up, holding
your gaze.

"Your room is okay, Molly?" asks Pasquale, popping up the
stairs. You tell them it's great, but really they shouldn't have
given you the best room, you're only staying one night. You
can find another place. Fabio turns his hands up in a helpless
gesture.

"One night, Laura?" he asks. "How can you stay in a place like
this for only one night?" You come down a few stairs and mum-
ble that you have to take the boat the next night, you have to get
home. Fabio and Pasquale argue with you, saying it is impossible
for you to leave so soon.

"*È cosí,*" you say. It's like that. It crosses your mind, though,
that it doesn't have to be like that. Maybe you could stay. These
two—well, especially Fabio—might turn out to be a lot of fun.
You could change your ticket. But you feel guilty about abandoning the professor.

You go to your separate rooms. You arrange your things, sit
out on the balcony in the sun, and hear Fabio calling you. He
comes up from the lower terrace with a pomegranate he's just
picked from an overhanging branch of the tree next door.

"Here," he says, handing you the fruit, "you can be Persephone."

You thank him, biting into the red rind. You are trying to remember who Persephone was. You pop a few of the juicy, tart seeds into your mouth.

"Now you *have* to stay," Fabio says, giving you a wicked smile.

Then you remember the myth, where Persephone, kidnapped from her island of Sicily by Hades, is forced to stay in the underworld because she ate some pomegranate seeds with which he tempted her. "Sorry," you say, tossing the pomegranate back into the neighbor's yard. But there are worse versions of hell, you think, than staying on Stromboli with Fabio.

Pasquale bellows from below that it is time to eat lunch, and he's already figured out the best place to eat. You whirl away from Fabio, and you all go to the pizzeria Da Luciano up the street.

Pasquale and Fabio greet the stout, graying owner effusively, and when Luciano tells them he is from Napoli, they practically embrace him. "We're southern Italians, from Puglia," says Fabio. "We'll feel right at home." As they saunter to your table, you're glad to be with them, thinking you'll probably get a better meal than the group of Germans sitting at the next table.

Pasquale opens his menu with relish. He orders the works: *primo, secondo, contorno*—pasta, swordfish, salad. He asks if anyone else is having wine, and you say just a drop, you have to climb the volcano today.

Fabio frowns. "Today? Why do you have to climb the volcano today?"

You explain that you have to leave tomorrow and absolutely must climb the volcano.

"Molly," says Pasquale. "Don't act so German. You need to relax for at least a day or two before you can even *think* about climbing a volcano." That settled, he orders a liter of wine.

You spread your arms in a helpless gesture, and order a salad and a plate of the pasta Stromboliana, homemade tagliatelle with roasted eggplant, capers, and fresh ricotta.

When the salad arrives—tiny, sweet cherry tomatoes, onions, and more capers—Pasquale begins asking questions, starting with how old you are. You ask him to guess, and he says twenty-five. Fabio rolls his eyes; even he thinks this is taking the gallant, flirtatious Italian man act a little too far. "But she has a baby face," Pasquale protests, pinching your cheek. You give him a look that says there will be no more pinching of cheeks. You ask how old they are: thirty-five. You tell them you are older than they are, so Fabio renames you Zia Laura, Aunt Laura, which Pasquale immediately changes to Zia Molly.

Pasquale asks if you are married.

"Divorced." They are fascinated; they don't come across many divorced people. Pasquale says he's married, but Fabio is single.

"Why?" If they're going to ask personal questions, so are you.

"Laura," Fabio says sorrowfully, "I have never met the right woman."

"Fabio," says Pasquale, "you have met plenty of the right women. Just too many at the same time."

Fabio ignores him, and Pasquale presses for details about your divorce.

"There's not much to the story," you tell them. "It just didn't work out."

"But you were *married*," says Pasquale.

"Not for long, and it was a long time ago."

Pasquale frowns. "Who decided to break up, you or him?" he asks.

Fabio flicks him on the arm. *"Basta,"* he says. "Don't ask her so many questions."

"Who cares? We're just a couple of guys she ran into," says Pasquale.

"It's okay," you say, picking at a piece of bread on the table. "We were married for a year and a half. Then he left me. For another woman."

They're quiet. Then Pasquale smacks his hand on the table. *"Porca miseria,"* he says. "That guy had to have been *crazy,* to leave you for someone else."

Fabio nods in agreement. *"Figlio di puttana."*

"You must have wanted to *kill* him," says Pasquale.

"You guys are southern Italians," you joke, spreading your arms. "Got any connections?"

Pasquale rubs his hands together gleefully. Fabio shoots him a look.

"I'm sorry, Laura," Fabio says, serious now. "You don't deserve what happened to you."

You shrug. "In the end, he did me a favor. I'm a lot better off. Now I can travel and have lunch with charming southern Italian men." You clink glasses with them. *"Cin cin."*

After an espresso, you go to the beach. Fabio spreads a towel out for you, then sits himself down on the pebbly black sand. "There's plenty of room," you say, moving over on the towel. Pasquale raises one of his big black eyebrows in your direction. You turn over and snooze, then wake up with a swim. You notice it's getting late in the afternoon, and announce that you are going to go climb the volcano. Pasquale rolls over in the sand, shading his eyes with his hand so he can have a better view of the mountain. "Molly," he says, "you don't want to go climb that thing now. It's twenty-four hundred meters high. Go back to sleep."

It does look like a long way up. But you'll be mad at yourself later if you come home from Stromboli without having climbed the volcano just so you could nap a little longer. You tell them you'll go find a guide.

"Laura," says Fabio, "Why do you need a guide to climb up a mountain? They take thirty thousand lire to show you how to put one foot in front of the other."

"I can't go by myself," you say. It is, after all, a live volcano, lava and all. You wouldn't want to take the wrong turn.

"Let us be your guides," says Fabio. "We climb mountains together all the time."

"Yeah," says Pasquale. "Only we aren't going today."

"It's okay, guys," you say, picking up your things. "I'm leaving. I'll wave to you from the top."

"If we leave now," Pasquale grudgingly calculates, staring up at the sky, "we'll just be there by sunset."

"*Va bene,*" says Fabio, rolling up the towel. "Let's take her."

"*Siete tanto gentili,*" you tell them. Such gentlemen.

You change at the *pensione,* have another quick espresso, and walk up to the piazza, where townspeople are milling about, sitting on the stone walls that overlook the sea. You keep going on the tiny road, too narrow for automobiles—which are banned, anyway—past square white houses with pastel doors and pocket-sized vineyards. There is a carnation-colored stucco house with a small plaque in front that commemorates the love affair the

Italian film director Roberto Rossellini had there with Ingrid Bergman while they were making the film *Stromboli*. You stare at it. You wish you had plaques nailed up around San Francisco to honor your past loves. After breaking up, after all the layers of bitterness laid over those sweet memories, it would be nice if at least there were a shiny bronze plaque somewhere saying that, for a while, you were in love, and that in itself is worth commemorating.

Fabio plucks a flower hanging over a stone wall and offers it to you with a flourish. You breathe in its fragrance and attach it to your day pack. You continue around the perimeter of the island. The road turns into a rocky dirt path as it starts up the mountain, and then into a narrow trail in a field of high grasses.

Fabio notices that you've lost the flower he's given you. "You Americans aren't very romantic," he says. "First you throw away the pomegranate, now the flower." You apologize, saying it was beautiful, so sweet, you don't know how it fell off. Pasquale gives Fabio a look and Fabio laughs; maybe he was fooling you, turning you in circles, and maybe not.

The trail snakes up the side of the mountain until you can see the smoking crater of the volcano. You climb higher and higher on switchbacks, and the trail becomes steep and rocky. You're slipping on the rocks and think that the next time you pack for a trip and there's a chance you'll climb a volcano, you won't take the hiking boots out at the last minute, thinking the black sneakers will do in a pinch, especially since they look okay with skirts. Every trip you go on, you have a shoe crisis. You go out and buy comfortable, rugged walking shoes you think you can wear with skirts, and then realize the Italians won't even let you into the country with those shoes, they're so ugly. What Italian woman has ever worn sport shoes with a skirt? Who buys shoes *before* they get to Italy, anyway?

"Have you ever seen a mountain like this one?" asks Pasquale, wiping his forehead with a handkerchief. You're embarrassed that with all this scenery around you, you are retroactively obsessing about which shoes to pack.

You look around and notice the steep cone, the grasses, the view of the houses below, the sea beyond. It is beautiful, you tell them, but, really, it isn't a mountain. It's a hill. You grew up in the part of the United States with the most mountains, Colorado, and the mountains there are something like five thousand meters, with snow on top that never melts. Fabio says he'd like to visit such a place, and asks if they can come stay with you, and you'll show them around. Sure, you say, sometime, and add that the thing they should really see is the Grand Canyon, because the landscape there is nothing like anything you'd ever find in Italy. Deep canyons, red rocks you can climb on, all colors of pink and orange and vermilion in fantastic-shaped stones. They promise to one day show up at your doorstep.

You stop, pant, and drink up most of the water, even though you're only about a third of the way to the top. This is rough going, native Coloradan or not. There is something decidedly unfriendly about the mountain. Maybe it's the sparse vegetation and the sheer sides. Maybe it's that the volcano threatens death and destruction every fifteen minutes. The townspeople seem to be full of reckless denial in face of the eventual certainty of natural disaster. Not unlike San Franciscans.

The higher you go, the faster Fabio and Pasquale scramble, determined to get to the top by sunset. You come to the part of the mountain where the bushes disappear and only slippery grayish pink rock remains, and you have to climb hand over foot to get up the cliffs. This is probably the fastest way up, but perhaps not the way the guides go. Finally you arrive at a knife-edged ridge that drops to a crumbly slope on one side, certain death below. Across the other side is the active crater, smoking, with a sheer lava field, the Sciara del Fuoco, channeling down to the sea. It is a barren moonscape with a smoky smell, fuming geysers, and loud rumblings.

You keep climbing on the jagged ridge, and all of a sudden you're near the top. You make your way to an overlook, level with the crater of the volcano.

"We're safe, here, right?" you ask Pasquale.

He shrugs. "It's only really blown once, in the 1930s. Most of the islanders escaped by boat, but then the tidal waves got them."

"Thanks," you say.

"We're fine," says Fabio. "Everyone comes here."

The sun is just settling into the sea and the sky is glowing pink. You stare at the smoking crater and all of a sudden, miraculously, it spews bright orange cinders into the rosy sky, a fierce eruption. Startled, you grab Fabio's hand. The fiery magma flows down the side of the mountain and booms, distantly, when the scalding lava hits the sea.

Pasquale walks up the ridge to take some photos. Fabio turns to you. "Are you okay?" he asks.

"Sure," you say. "That was amazing."

He examines your hand like it's a foreign object, then turns it over and places a kiss on your palm.

Going down in the dark is much harder, even with flashlights. You pass several large groups with guides climbing up, everyone in hard hats and carrying walking sticks. You wish you'd been able to climb the mountain fifteen years before, as the professor had, and hardly seen a soul. You can see why he never wants to return.

When the trail levels out, Pasquale, in front of you, wants to practice his English. You start with a few phrases, like "nice to meet you," and "the pleasure is mine." Impatient, he wants to know how to say Italy's most notorious epithet.

"Forget it, it's too vulgar," you say.

"Forget it," he repeats. Then he stops and turns around on the trail. "Molly, I'm not a cretin. Say *vaffanculo.*"

You sigh. "Stick it up your ass," you say.

"Stick 'em up!" Pasquale crows. He'd heard that one before, in movies. "Stick 'em up your ass!" He's trundling down the trail, yelling the phrase at top volume. Some of the hikers coming up the other way appear to be alarmed. You shush him, and say it isn't very nice.

"Can you say that in New York?" he asks.

"In New York, that could get you into a lot of trouble," you say. "Plus, it's a little too graphic, and they don't use it much there."

"Well, what do they use?" he asks. "Come on, Molly."

"Fuck," you concede.

He tries that out. "Fuck, fuck, fuck!" He smacks his lips. "That's a good one. That one makes a really strong sound."

He asks how it is used, and you explain that it is most often a simple expletive, or a verb in the imperative form, but that it is actually quite grammatically versatile—an adjective, noun, verb, whatever you want. "The view from the volcano was fucking incredible," you tell him, by way of example. "Fuck! I hit my toe!"

Fabio, ahead of you and out of earshot, gives a gesture asking what the hell is going on back there.

Pasquale, awed that one word can say so much so obscenely, tries out some sentences. Finally you work up to making an entire sentence out of the word. "Fuck! We're fucked, you fucking fuck!"

He clambers down the hill. "Fucking great! Fucking fuck! Stick 'em up the fuck!" He pulls out his *telefonino* and calls his wife, telling her at length that he's on the volcano and learning English, which, once you know a few key words, is really easy.

Fabio, stopped at the volcano observatory, rolls his eyes at Pasquale and his *telefonino*. You all go into the bar, drink a liter of water each, and continue on the road into town, which seems to stretch for miles. It's completely dark, with no street lights. Walking three abreast in the starlight, Fabio starts reciting a poem. It's about a woman named Sylvia, whose beauty flashed in splendor from eyes which laughed and yet were hidden. When he finishes, you compliment him and ask the name of the poet. Pasquale and Fabio are amazed you don't know Giacomo Leopardi, one of the greatest Italian lyric poets of the nineteenth century. It's like saying you'd never heard of William Shakespeare, or at least Walt Whitman.

They want you to recite a poem, and you tell them you're ashamed to say that the only ones you know by heart are the one you read at your wedding, a Philip Larkin poem, and a cowboy poem you learned in sixth grade. They want to hear the wedding poem, but you tell them it's sad; it's by a cynical and pessimistic English poet, who never married, about whether love was for now or for always, whether it was a mirage or a miracle—and then, in fact, it did turn out to be an illusion.

"Laura," says Fabio. "You read a poem like that at your wedding? You Americans *really* aren't very romantic."

"It seemed romantic at the time," you say. "I thought a poem that asked if love was for now or for always was a way of saying that the romance of the present could continue in a marriage over time, that always would be always now, that all those wonderful moments in the present would, in the end, add up to something more eternal. And my ex-husband loved that poet."

Fabio cocks his head. "What did he read?" he asks.

He had recited a poem his grandfather wrote, and then talked about how, when you first met at a party, you told him it was like traveling, where you could say anything to a stranger. At the wedding he said he didn't have the feeling of traveling when he met you; he had the feeling, finally, of being home.

"Not bad," says Fabio. "That's pretty romantic."

Pasquale lets out an exasperated noise. "You know what I think about that guy?" He pauses for effect. "Stick 'em up the fuck."

"Recite the poem from the cowboys," Fabio asks, ignoring Pasquale. You recite it, and they listen respectfully, not understanding a word, commenting that they especially like the whoopee-ti-yi-yo part. Do you know another one?

"Does Bob Dylan count as poetry?"

"No," says Pasquale definitively. They seem a bit appalled at your meager showing.

"Did you go to university?" asks Fabio cautiously, glancing sideways at Pasquale.

Of course, you assure him, a good one. You just never memorized any poetry.

This is beyond his comprehension. "If you don't know any

poems, what do you do when you don't have a book?" You've never thought about it that way. You guess if you were really stuck somewhere, in a little fishing village like Ingrid Bergman's character in *Stromboli,* you would indeed wish you knew some poetry to keep you company.

"I dream about Italy," you reply.

Fabio smiles.

"Tell the truth," says Pasquale. "You dream about Italian *men.*"

The next day, after another morning at the beach, you offer to treat them—they were, after all, your guides up the mountain—but they refuse. "We'll make you a real Mediterranean lunch," says Pasquale. "Something to remember us by."

"What a pleasure," you say. "You know how to cook?"

"Sure," says Pasquale. "In an emergency."

"Who does all the cooking at your house?"

Pasquale looks at you like you're crazy. "My wife, of course."

"Why don't you cook sometimes?"

Pasquale puts his hands together in a prayer gesture. "The kitchen is her world," he says. "Men have one world, and women have another. You don't mess with a thing like that."

"Pasquale," you say, uncertain, all of a sudden, that a southern Italian man is such a good idea, "have you ever heard of feminism? Men cook a little here, women cook a little there?"

"Don't get the wrong impression," says Fabio, "it's just him."

"It's not the men's fault!" says Pasquale. "You go into an Italian woman's kitchen, she comes after you with a knife."

Fabio turns to you. "Who cooked in your house when you were married?"

You pause.

"*She* did," says Pasquale, smacking the air in your direction. "She never let her husband anywhere *near* the kitchen."

"Well," you say. "He did the dishes."

"*Un punto!*" says Pasquale, scoring one for himself.

You look at Fabio. "And you?"

"I cook," says Fabio. "I'm a pretty good cook."

"You wouldn't *have* to cook if you were married," says Pasquale. Fabio scowls.

"So many good girls you've passed up," says Pasquale. "Patrizia, Alessandra. Cristina! You should have married Cristina, she was a nice girl, and she loved you."

This is clearly a long-running discussion. "I want something more," says Fabio, gazing out into the distance. "Someone who's seen more of the world than the little town she grew up in. Someone exciting, full of ideas."

"What do you know?" Pasquale asked, sweeping a wide arc of sand in front of him. "You're thirty-five years old already. You're not a kid anymore. You're luckier than most guys and you throw it all away."

"I don't just want a nice little house with a wife in the kitchen," says Fabio.

"You'll end up all alone, with your skinny cat, both of you eating plain noodles," says Pasquale.

"Laura," says Fabio, ignoring him. "Come stay with me in southern Italy and I will cook for you every day."

"Let's see how you do with lunch."

They leave to go shopping, and you take a shower; the last one, you realize, until you're back in San Francisco. Unless you're going to change your ticket and stay on Stromboli. You don't know. You've climbed the volcano. You don't want to leave the professor stranded on the boat. But now there's a new distraction.

You look at the palm of your hand, where he had kissed it. So tempting. You pack your things anyway, stuffing bags of fresh capers into your shoes, hoping Customs won't find them there.

You leave the *pensione* to buy some wine and when you return Fabio and Pasquale are laboring over their lunch plans and shouting at each other. You peek into the tiny kitchen, and Pasquale shoos you out. Then he elbows Fabio out of the way to get to the sink. The only dining table is in your room, so you go up there, open all the shutters, spread a fresh sheet on the table, and pick a few flowers from the terrace to put in a water glass in the middle. The sun comes streaming in to the table.

Pasquale eventually comes upstairs with a loaf of bread, wine, silverware, and grunts his approval. He returns with a big saucepan full of pasta and some bowls, and shouts down at Fabio to come. Fabio appears, carrying a tomato, caper, and tuna salad. "Very nice," he says, admiring the table.

Pasquale serves out the pasta—roasted red peppers with onions, olive oil, and fresh ricotta. "This is fabulous," you say. Pasquale looks proud. "A real Mediterranean dish."

"It's a little oily," says Fabio. He glances around the room, taking in your packed luggage. "Laura, why do you have to leave?"

You shrug.

Pasquale registers that his friend is looking a little hurt. "She's just a rich, spoiled American girl," he says. "What can you expect?"

This surprises you. "Pasquale," you say, "that's not fair."

"Well, it's true," he says. "You come all the way here from the United States just to climb the volcano, and then you leave."

You put down your fork and stop chewing. Now you really are ready to leave.

"Come on," says Fabio, touching your arm. "Pasquale didn't mean to insult you. "We tease each other all the time."

"I was kidding. Even if I had said something that made you feel bad, you could have just teased me back," says Pasquale. He thinks for a second. "Hey, Molly, try repeating that." He says the complicated, multitense phrase again.

You gamely attempt to repeat it, subjunctive tenses and all, and feel a little better.

"How do you like it when she speaks really good Italian?" Pasquale asks Fabio. "You know, Molly, I love it when you speak good Italian, but I love it more when you make mistakes." He reaches to pinch your cheek, and for once, you let him.

"Now give me a little kiss," Pasquale says, offering his cheek. "We're friends." You air kiss him on one cheek, then the other. He puts his hand to his cheek and then clutches his heart. "Now give him a kiss," he says, gesturing to Fabio. You turn your cheek to Fabio, but he catches your chin and turns it back so he can kiss you, briefly but wetly, on the lips. He has such soft lips.

"All better?" asks Pasquale.

You nod.

"Let's have some malvasia, *bella*," says Fabio. He opens the sweet dessert wine, pours it, and inhales the aroma from his glass.

"To our lovely American friend," he says. "May we see her again soon."

"To Zia Molly," says Pasquale.

"To my Italian friends," you say. "I hope you'll come visit me."

You drink a glass of the fortified wine and soon the room is almost blurry in its dreaminess.

"Facciamo un pisolino," says Pasquale. Let's take a little nap.

He goes over to your bed and lies down heavily. You protest that it is your bed, and he has to go downstairs. "I can't make it downstairs, Molly," he says, curling over onto his side. "Leave me alone."

You try pushing and cajoling him to move, but he won't budge. "I'm sleeping," he says. "You can sleep here next to me, or you can go sleep downstairs. I don't care." You're sleepy, too. You've become accustomed to the Italian habit of having a big lunch and a little snooze in the afternoon. You glance over to Fabio for some assistance in moving Pasquale off your bed, but he shrugs his shoulders helplessly.

"You can have Pasquale's bed," he says, getting up and clearing the rest of the dishes.

"I don't want Pasquale's bed," you say, following him downstairs.

He goes into the bedroom and smooths out the cover on Pasquale's bed. "There. You have a little nap. I'm going outside." It was gentlemanly of him to leave you by yourself to nap, so you spread out and close your eyes.

Half an hour later you hear Fabio tiptoe back into the darkened room. He hands you a piece of paper and then lies down on his bed against the wall. You open the paper; it's a poem. It compares you to malvasia, sweet and inebriating. But the American in you, it says, is confused about being a woman. Tender and genteel, a pleasure to encounter, with a hidden heat and sweet humor. *"Ricorda e non dimenticare, non è mai sbagliato amare."*

Remember and don't forget that it's never wrong to love. It all sounds much better in Italian.

You fold the paper and put it in your pocket. No one has ever written a poem for you—not even the writer you dated, who'd gotten a fellowship for his poetry. You get up, go over to Fabio's bed, and lean over to give him a little kiss on the cheek. "That was incredibly sweet," you tell him. He kisses you back on the lips, and then again. His lips are as soft as you imagined. He pulls you down on top of him and kisses you some more, running his hands up and down your back, stroking your cheeks and hair. He has such a smooth body and nice touch that you lose thought of everything in a malvasia haze.

Fabio eventually comes up for air and inspects your arm, which is covered with no-see-um bites. "You're bitten all over!" he says. He kisses your arm all the way down to your pinkie finger with its bandage. "And here, what's this?"

"*La murena*," you say drunkenly.

He kisses your pinkie finger. "Everything bites you because you are so appetizing."

He gives you a little nibble on your neck. *"Ti mordo,"* he says. I'll bite you.

You squeal. He covers your mouth with his hand. "Shhh!" he says, pointing upstairs to where Pasquale is sleeping. *"Ti mordo,"* he whispers fiercely. He bites you again lightly on your collarbone and he covers your mouth with his hand again, shushing you. "You're delicious," he says. He nibbles you on your ribs, your waist, your bellybutton, your inner thigh, and then he starts licking you between nibbles.

The last thing in the world you want is for him to stop. You have to leave soon, though, to meet the professor. Or you could stay. You know that if you don't stop right now, it'll all be over. You won't make it to the boat to wave good-bye to the professor, and you have to at least wave good-bye. "Fabio," you say, finally sitting upright, stopping to catch your breath.

"Fabio," you say, touching his curls, and pulling his face close to yours. "I don't think I can do this right now."

He considers that. "If you don't want to make love, there are a lot of other things we could do." He suggests several possibilities.

"You're such a good Catholic boy," you say, and uncoil one of his ringlets like a spring. "You know all the alternatives." You let the curl go. "I can't, but really, I wish I could."

"So don't leave," he says.

"I'm meeting my friend on the boat."

"You're meeting this guy tonight? On the boat?" he asks. He frowns and rolls over onto his back.

"Yes," you say. "I told you that yesterday."

He crosses his arms in front of him.

"Come on, Fabio," you say, holding one of his cheeks with your hand. "Let's go take a walk while there's still light."

You walk down to the beach, where you find some big flat rocks and play at jumping from one to another without getting wet.

"Stay," calls Fabio from another rock. "We haven't had a chance to get to know each other." He holds out his hand for you as you jump over to his rock. He pulls you close to him. "Just stay."

What would it hurt to stay, really? Maybe Fabio has some potential—at the very least, for a few days. At least he isn't married. Not that a southern Italian music teacher is necessarily a great prospect, but who knows? You haven't really given him a chance. And you could still wave good-bye to the professor, you wouldn't miss him entirely.

"Okay," you finally say. "I'll see what I can do. I'll call my travel agent."

He walks back to the *pensione* while you go to the telephone booth near the port and make the call. You really have no reason to leave the islands to go back home. Your travel agent answers, six thousand miles away, clicking away at his computer, and finally tells you that he can change the ticket, if you want to leave five days later. Should he do it?

"Yes," you say. You're watching a boat pull in to the harbor. "Well, wait." You finger the blue shirt you're wearing, the professor's frayed shirt. And somehow you can't do it. You need to be with the professor, even if only for a few hours in a crowded cabin on a boat. It's more important than five days on Stromboli with Fabio. You can't quite take Fabio seriously, and you just aren't ready to wave good-bye to the professor for good. "No," you tell the travel agent. "I'm sorry. Sorry to bother you."

You go to the store and automatically buy a picnic for the professor, too. The man at the cash register, once he hears you speak Italian, flirts with you a little, explaining that the volcano on the island arouses passions in lovers. You smile and tell him you will be sure to tell your husband that, and gather up your neatly tied packages.

At the *pensione*, Pasquale is talking on his *telefonino* with his wife. You tell Fabio it was impossible to change your ticket. "I'm sorry," you say, and give him a little hug. You go upstairs for your bag.

Fabio, disappointed, walks you to the port, and sits on the dock while you spot the ship in the distance, finally pulling in. A man on board tosses a thick white rope to a man on shore, who secures it. The large metal gangway is lowered, revealing cars and passengers ready to disembark. In the corner you see the familiar figure of the professor. You resist waving for Fabio's sake, and smile at M. The professor gives a gesture asking whether you are on the boat or off, and you nod, you're coming. He turns around and disappears into the belly of the boat.

Pasquale, still on his *telefonino*, catches up with you. He stands there chatting and then finally hangs up. He puts out his hand. "Give my greetings to California, Molly," he says abruptly, and leaves you alone.

Fabio gives you a long kiss on the lips, and a hug. "I hope I see you again," he says. "I'm going to think about you often when I'm alone." You get lost in his kiss. You're still tempted to turn around and walk away with him. You half wonder if the professor could see you, but you doubt it. He was the one, anyway, who told you to go find an Italian boyfriend.

"You're great," you tell Fabio, finally pulling away. "Write to me. Send me another poem." You squeeze his hand and walk aboard the boat, resisting the urge to turn around.

You haul your bag up to the deck and look around for the professor. He's sitting on top of a lifejacket container, smoking. You give him a hug.

"It seems like it's been a long time," he says.

"Yes," you say. "A lot has happened in two days."

"It looks like a lot has happened. You've made good progress. You found yourself a little *storia*," he says, leering. And then after a pause, "He was handsome."

"He was all right," you say. "Just a couple of guys I met. They were entertaining."

You show the professor the picnic you've brought. He barely glances at it. "I've eaten," he says.

"Oh," you say, disappointed, and pull out a little bread and ricotta. "Fresh ricotta," you say. "Not even a bite? A glass of wine?"

"Nothing," he says. He sits there smoking and watches Stromboli get smaller behind you.

"Did you see me?" asks the professor.

"I saw you when the boat first pulled up," you say. "You saw me, too."

"No, after that," he says.

"You went inside," you say.

He's quiet. "That was quite a nice kiss good-bye."

"I'm sorry," you say. "I thought you were inside. It was no big deal."

"No, no," he says. "Good for you. Maybe you should have stayed with him."

"I wanted to see you," you say.

You sit there in silence for a while, uneasily, and then you start chattering about your two days on Stromboli. You tell him all about climbing the volcano, and how he was lucky he didn't go back there because of the long line of tourists making their way up with guides.

"I know," he says curtly.

You watch the volcano, vaguely outlined against the dark sea, hoping it will erupt.

"Come on," the professor says to the volcano. "Say good-bye to us." But the volcano remains calm.

"No show tonight," you say. "A pity."

"Yes," he says, yawning. "I'm tired."

It's getting cold, and you go below deck to your cabin. You

notice the professor has left a small bottle of wine for you in the room, and you thank him. He undresses, and gives you a little kiss. "No," he says, almost to himself. He climbs right up to his bunk. *"Buona notte, cara,"* he says.

"Buona notte," you say, confused. You can't sleep, so you go back out on deck, breathing in the moist, cool air. You feel like you've betrayed the professor, and hurt his feelings. You can't believe he's so cold to you, that he doesn't want to make love to you, that your trip will end this way.

You go back down to the cabin and climb into your bunk. In a few moments, the professor joins you. "I can't resist you," he says. You make love, but it is perfunctory; you don't open your eyes or kiss each other on the lips. Then he goes back to his bunk without a word.

The boat arrives in Naples early, and you wake to a knock on the door. You have to gather your things together quickly, with barely time for a cappuccino before the boat pulls into the harbor in Naples. On deck, the professor paces from one side to another, surveying the harbor. You disembark, and walk quietly from the berth to the port entrance, where taxis are waiting.

"You should have plenty of time to make your plane," he says.

You nod, and ask him what he's going to do in Naples that day.

"The museum of archaeology, of course," he says. As if you needed to ask.

He hails a taxi, opens the door for you, and places your bag in the back seat.

You hand him a bottle of malvasia without a word. He gives you a brief kiss on each cheek.

"Ciao," he says absently. *"Adieu."* And he swings the door shut.

{TEN}

MOROCCO

You're glad, for once, to be home. You don't think or talk much about your vacation with the professor, because when you do, something lands with a thud in the pit of your stomach. Did you ruin your relationship with M. over a silly kiss with an Italian man you barely knew? After all those wonderful times together, would you never see each other again?

You start so many letters to him, and even pick up the phone once or twice to call Paris, but you don't know what to say. He was the one who suggested you try to find another Italian lover. You thought he hadn't really cared. And now you've hurt him, so stupidly.

For more than two years, you've relied on the professor, or the thought of him, to keep you from sinking into loneliness. You've been able to stand being single in San Francisco because in the back of your mind you knew you had another world of romance you could return to in just a matter of months. However distant, however infrequently you saw him, you had a lover.

But now that world, that lover, has disappeared into a series of memories and photographs.

And yet, the professor stays with you. He's with you when you decide to take a little extra care to cook a meal for yourself, and then call up a friend on a whim to come share it. He's there when you realize you have to stop being so bored with your work and dive into something different, something you can feel passionate about again. He comes along when you go shopping for clothes that make you feel pretty. He pushes you to get out, go to parties, check out art exhibits, take dance classes, and strike up conversations with strangers. Some of his amusement about the world has rubbed off on you, along with a zest for pleasure that just tilts toward excess. You have been his student in the fine art of *joie de vivrism,* and now you are on your own.

You aren't going to think of yourself as so self-consciously single any more, a divorcée, hunting for Mr. Right. You don't want to go through life as if there were a big gaping hole in it, as if everything was fine except for this big realm of unspeakable sadness. So you stop talking about your ex-husband, your divorce, and your sorry single state. You let go of worrying about whether you are going to have a child someday. If a really great man happens along in your life—wonderful. If you end up having a child, then that will be another adventure. And if not—no husband, no baby—you are still going to be just fine. Most of the time, you believe that.

Then, more than two months later, the professor sends you a note. "I'm sorry if, even though we're lovers, I'm sometimes cold to you," he says. "It's nothing. I kiss you everywhere."

Relieved, you write him back. You don't apologize for kissing Fabio on the dock, because the professor would be offended to think you believed that had bothered him. "I have a deep affection for you, and I love spending time with you, if you like," you write. "If not, then I'll always have wonderful memories of our time together. You've taught me so much about pleasure, and it has changed me forever." You want to give the professor a graceful out if he needs it.

Again, you don't hear from him. Then at the New Year, he sends you a card with a woodblock illustration of a volcano erupting. "I wish a sea of happiness and contentment for you in the future," he says, "and somewhere in that sea I hope there will always be a little island for us and our *bella vita*."

He writes again about a month later and asks if you will be free in February. So it really isn't over. You'll see him again.

You write back: New Orleans? New York City? Cuba? You are ready to go anywhere to see him.

"Morocco," he writes. A place you've always hoped to visit.

The international flight from New York to Morocco lands in Casablanca. The word "Casablanca" brings to mind intrigue and romance, a place where ceiling fans spin slowly over steamy bars, elegant former lovers toss off heartbreaking remarks, and sex and danger smolder just beneath the surface. But the real Casablanca, the professor assured you when you were making plans, isn't so charming. It's a chaotic town, full of messy traffic and hastily constructed concrete buildings, the no-nonsense economic center of Morocco, where the only thing called "Rick's Cafe" is a drink at the Hyatt. He doesn't want to go near there.

But since you are nervous about being alone in Morocco, he agrees to meet you in Casablanca anyway, and then you'll take the train together to Fez.

Because of a flight snafu, you arrive in Casablanca two days before you are supposed to meet the professor. You make your way to the hotel where he's made a reservation, and the manager seems surprised to see you. You hang around the lobby long enough, without surrendering your passport and credit card, to realize why. The professor, always on the lookout for the inexpensive, somewhat rundown but still charming hotels in the old part of town, has accidentally booked you into a bordello. Businessmen keep arriving with heavily madeup women, and no one has any bags. Interesting as the scene is, you don't like the way you're being eyed, so you consult your guidebook, and hail a taxi to drive you to a four-star hotel (still cheap by American standards), with no hookers in sight.

There, you're somewhat at a loss. You're uneasy being alone in a country where you don't speak the language and where single, unveiled women travelers aren't exactly treated warmly. You don't want to simply hole up in an American-style hotel while you wait for the professor, ordering room service, so you decide to try to seek out the company of some women. You had met a few local flight attendants on the plane out, so you give them a call. One invites you over to her house for couscous the next day, and then insists you go to the *hammam*—the women's baths—afterward. You spend the afternoon at some huge marble baths, covered in black gooey soap, having your skin rubbed and massaged, seeing what goes on in the world hidden away from Western eyes, the women's world beneath their djellabahs.

Back at the hotel, you worry that the professor won't find you, that he hasn't gotten the message you asked one of the

Moroccan women to leave for him at the first hotel. You don't know whether the man at the bordello will pass along a message without a tip. But finally the professor calls, and soon he is knocking on your door, and then hugging you.

"Look at us," he says, pulling back to see you. "We have become old lovers."

"Speak for yourself," you say. It is always so exciting to see him again, as much of an electric thrill as the first time you saw him again after Ischia, in Milano.

He holds you, and kisses you, and whatever anxiety was between you, whatever coldness you felt the last time you were together, dissolves. You're just happy to see each other again, immediately comfortable. You are, in fact, old lovers by now.

You leave the hotel to walk around the city, where, accompanied by a man who speaks French, you no longer feel so obviously out of place. You find a traditional Moroccan restaurant, with a courtyard and a tapestried dining room with low cushiony seats. You order a panache of salads, spread out before you with spicy olives and rich bread on a round brass platter. The professor insists you try a pigeon pastilla. Like any urban dweller, you are wary of eating pigeon, but you give it a try. It is a succulent dish of tender bird and ground almonds nestled inside layers of phyllo dough, sprinkled with cinnamon and powdered sugar on the top, a real delicacy.

You drink some of the sweet Moroccan wine. "Okay, *signorina*," the professor says. *"Raccontami tutto."* Tell me about your love life.

After your last parting, with Fabio, you wouldn't tell him about another man. Anyway, as it turns out, there isn't one. And that's just fine.

"Oh, I can't keep up," you tease him. "Which one?"

He raises an eyebrow.

"I've been hibernating," you say. "There were a couple of possibilities, men I probably could've had a little story with, but I just didn't feel like jumping into bed with them, having casual sex."

"Why not?" he asks. "You meet someone sexy, you sleep with him, so what?"

"A comfort, not a pleasure," you say. "It's like eating fast food. You aren't hungry anymore, but you feel terrible afterward."

"I don't know about that," says the professor, smiling to himself.

"Well, you're a man. But I'm not sleeping with anyone again who doesn't really care about me, who doesn't have an open heart. Not that I have to marry him, but it has to be sweet."

The professor squeezes your hand. "You are sweet, my dear."

"You're not just saying that to get me into bed, are you?"

"Maybe," he says.

The next morning, you pack your things and make your way to the train station. You study the schedules and find that it will be a long wait for the train to Fez, where you had planned to go. A train leaves for Marrakesh in fifteen minutes, so you take that instead. You board the train and watch the sparse, reddish landscape roll by, drowsily, until you pull in, four hours later, to Marrakesh.

At first glance, Marrakesh isn't the exotic place you expected it to be, the crossroads of international vagabonds, hippie travelers, and traders. You arrive in the new part of town, the Ville Nouvelle, which is hot and dusty, full of modern concrete buildings that have cafés with plastic tables and chairs out front. You find a decent but charmless hotel, eat some lunch, and then take a cab to the old section of town.

There, the ambiance changes completely, with high earthen walls, palm trees, and mazes of streets. The cabdriver lets you out at the huge central square in Marrakesh, the famed Djemā'a el-Fna, where the carnival atmosphere has drawn travelers since medieval times. Berber acrobats in grungy red uniforms do handsprings and flips in the center of a crowd. Veiled, barefoot girls come up, displaying photos of henna designs you can have painted on your hands or feet. Witchy-looking women sell medicinal herbs and dispense advice. Berber water-sellers in wide, round, tasseled hats clank as they walk by peddling glasses of water. The scene isn't all for tourists; there are throngs of locals gathered around storytellers, who are dramatically acting out their Arab tales.

You edge toward a snake charmer, who is playing a tune for a decidedly weary cobra. Fascinated and a little phobic, you take his photo. One of his assistants immediately comes up for a tip, which you give him. Then, perhaps hoping for a bigger tip, he gives you a close look at another snake, right in your face. You shriek and shoot off in the other direction, and the professor catches up with you, laughing.

You go to a restaurant overlooking the square for mint tea and watch the scene. As the day grows hotter, people disperse, and the square becomes almost deserted, except for the covered stands selling fresh-squeezed orange juice, tables piled high with almonds, dates, seeds, and figs. A few desultory musicians and jugglers circle the square.

You finish your tea and wander into the walled medina, the souk, where hundreds of colorful, crowded stalls sell pointy Moroccan babouche slippers, brass teapots, spices piled in richly hued pyramids, silver jewelry, housewares, fabric, chickens, pigs, all manner of things. The streets inside the medina are so narrow you can practically touch the walls on both sides at once. You take one route until the vendor stalls run out and you dead-end in a corner of a residential street, and then you turn around and take another until you end up in a square, where women are painting each other with minutely intricate henna designs. You get completely lost, but always find your way back. Young boys keep coming up, offering to be your guides, but the professor shoos them away in French.

You aren't hassled by the young Moroccans—they are put off by a good-humored refusal—but several times you feel someone pull a piece of your hair, which seems hostile. It isn't until you read anthropologist Elizabeth Fernea's book *A Street in Marrakesh* that you understand it isn't an aggressive act. Blond hair, she explains, is so unusual in northern Africa that Moroccans think it's full of "baraka," or good karma. Pulling a piece of baraka from a stranger's head is just a good luck charm, like plucking a four-leaf clover. It isn't aggressive, but it's a little hard to get used to.

You walk by an intriguing restaurant with Moroccan tiles, closed, promising "Haute Gastronomie Marocaine." Then you find your way to the jewelry area, where you have a mission, to buy a friend a necklace of large coral beads. You go from one shop to another, showing the beads you've brought with you to match, until you come to a small one deep inside the medina, where a boy strings together a beautiful strand of coral while you drink tea with the shop owner and the professor and he talk about Arab politics, how the Middle Eastern world will change with the recent succession of the Jordanian and Moroccan princes. You are lost with their French, and just watch the passersby.

Leaving the medina, you find an antique-rug shop. You enter a long, low-ceilinged corridor to the interior of the shop, which opens up into a large courtyard, where the balcony is draped with rugs of every shape and rich color, and huge Moroccan pottery pieces are propped up on the floor. The professor and you both light on the same rug, a small antique Berber prayer rug, naturally dyed red and blue. He bargains with them, has tea, bargains some more, and after about an hour, leaves with the rug for fifty dollars. You're jealous.

By the time you make it back out to the square, the acrobats and snake charmers have gone home, replaced by row after row of restaurants, grilling lamb kabobs, snails, and sheep's heads outdoors. You find a cab and cross town back to the new section, to another world.

The next day is your birthday. The professor wakes you with a beautiful package from a Paris boutique; it is a lovely Thai shawl, deep red and turquoise, the perfect colors. "You've made it difficult," you tell him, giving him a kiss. "Now I have to choose between two beautiful scarves you've given me." You put on your black travel dress and wrap the shawl around.

"*Bella,*" he says.

He suggests you spend the day exploring the gardens of Marrakesh. You start by seeing the outside of the Koutoubia Mosque, the seventy-meter-high monument in the middle of Marrakesh, built in the late twelfth century, but never open to non-Muslims. From there you walk to the Palais el-Badi, one of the grandest palaces in the late sixteenth century, now in ruins, except for a few empty swimming pools and a lot of storks nesting on the walls. You take a horse-drawn carriage from there to the Jardin Menara, outside of town. The professor loves clopping around in the carriage, because it reminds him of how he got around Cairo as a child, when his parents sometimes let him sit up front and take the reins.

You stroll around the Jardin Menara, a large, still pool with a pavilion in the back, and groves of olive trees with a view of the High Atlas Mountains beyond. From there, you go to the Hotel La Mamounia, a top-notch English-style hotel, with lovely gardens filled with orange trees. You sit together on the grounds and rest in the sun, holding hands. Your favorite garden is across town, the Jardin Majorelle, filled with lush flowers and plants, laid out by the French painter Jacques Majorelle, who lived there from 1922 to 1962. The villa is a deep cobalt blue, and the gardens are profusely green and refreshing. The professor is dreamy with the aesthetic pleasure of the place.

It has been a magical day. The professor asks where you want to eat dinner, and you think you should try the mysterious restaurant in the medina you spotted the day before. You take a cab as far into the medina as cars can go. The driver lets you out, and a young man dressed all in white appears, to lead you to the restaurant. You follow him from one labyrinthine alley to another, the medina looking so different at night, with everything closed. Finally you come to the door with the mosaic tiles. You enter the restaurant into a small foyer hung with thick burgundy drapes, where two men in fezzes sit, smoking *sheesha*— water pipes. They point you through the drapes, and you expect another tiny room. Instead, you enter into a palace, so much bigger and lighter than anything you could have imagined existed in the medina from the outside. You both gasp. There are thick red Persian carpets on the floor, rose petals strewn about, with blue Moroccan tiles and lacy white plasterwork on the walls. There is a carved and painted cedar ceiling with awnings, and Venetian lamps softly light the room. "Spectacular," you say, and the professor slowly nods his head.

You sit on low cushioned banquettes, and the waiters serve you the meal, with no menus, no prices. You only hope that since it is Morocco, the cost won't be exorbitant, but you don't care, it's too extraordinary. Musicians play in the center of the huge courtyard-like room. You have a pigeon pastilla, so delicate and savory, then a tender piece of lamb with lemons—you are glad, after enough time with the professor, that you decided being a vegetarian was too boring—and then a couscous, and, finally, for dessert a stack of crisp, delicate corn cakes with cream, which tastes, strangely, just like a bowl of corn flakes. The dinner is magical. The professor raises his glass of wine, looks you in the eyes, and wishes you a happy birthday.

"You know," he says, "this could be one of those sentimental moments."

"Yes," you say, and it is. You clink glasses and drink. There is no one you would rather be with at that moment, no place more exotic.

"But you never really let yourself be really sentimental with me," says the professor.

You sip your wine. You don't know what to say. You love the professor, you're crazy about him, but you know there are built-in limits—which is the only reason you'd been able to open your heart to him so soon after your divorce in the first place. Sometimes you fantasize that you could end up together, living on a beach in Italy or India with your pensions, reading books and playing chess and enjoying one perfect moment after another. But you know it's a fantasy. You just smile at him.

"It's good," he says. "I don't think I could stand it if you were sentimental. I suppose it would be too problematic, it would have to end."

"I don't mean to be so practical," you say. "But if I were sentimental about you, if I let myself completely fall in love with you, I would start thinking about learning French and moving to Paris and it would all be impossible."

"*Sì,*" he says. "*Sì.*" He turns his attention to the musicians, then back to you. "It is just nice to feel loved."

You take his hand and hold it across the table. "I love you as much as I can," you say.

"I know," says the professor. "We understand each other so well."

The waiter arrives with mint tea, pouring it into your glasses with flourish, from high in the air.

The professor sips his tea. He kisses you on the cheek. You sit quietly, taking in the atmosphere of the enchanted room, until your tea turns cold.

The next day, you rent a taxi to take you into the High Atlas Mountains outside of Marrakesh, the Ourika Valley. You are surprised at how the dry foothills look like New Mexico, with cactus, brush, and earth the color of dried blood. The only difference is the mud villages that cling to the sides of the hills. The valley is cool, and you stop for tea at a Berber village, overlook-

ing the river. You make your way to another village at the end
of the valley, where the mountains really start, where there is a
short hike to a waterfall. The professor isn't interested in hiking,
but you suggest that you at least stretch your legs.

When you travel together on islands, you always swim a lot,
and so never feel antsy about getting more exercise. But the professor can sense that you are a little restless, and apologizes. "It's
one of my defects," he says. "I'm just not very *sportif.*"

"I don't think it's a defect," you say. "You don't have any big
defects. It's just the way you are."

"I have plenty of defects," says the professor. "At least my
wife would say so."

"Really?" you ask. "Like what?"

The professor begins to list his defects. He is a little vain, he
says. He doesn't do well at dinner parties, doesn't like to make
chatty conversation. He dresses too hippie for his wife's taste.
He doesn't know how to fix anything around the house. He isn't
all that ambitious; if he were really rich, all he would do is travel
the world and stay at great hotels.

"None of those seem so bad to me," you say. If, in fact,
you were contemplating a long relationship with someone like
him, a few of those defects would bother you. The professor can
also be a little cheap sometimes, he infrequently pays you any
compliments, and he smokes too much. You suppose if you ran
across him in a personals ad, "Married professor, 51, smoker,
seeks discreet *rendez-vous* with younger woman who will split the
tab," you would pass him right by. But it's good for you to be
involved with someone, however sporadically, whose defects
you see but don't criticize. You just accept the professor for who
he is, and so there's very little tension. It makes you wonder why

you are so critical of the men you are in relationships with, that maybe you should go easy. When you let go of the expectation of marriage and happily-ever-after, you can just enjoy someone wholeheartedly for who they are. "Everyone has defects," you tell the professor. "It's just part of the package."

The professor agrees to take a little walk, and you make it up to a pretty waterfall, only twenty minutes. You know you would love to come back to Morocco with someone who would go trekking with you, but you are content to be with the professor.

"And you?" he asks. "What would your ex-husband say your defects are?"

"My ex-husband wouldn't be the best judge," you tell him. "I suppose he would say I am too impulsive, too excitable, and my boiling point is too low. What do you think?"

"Too dangerous," he says. "I'm not answering that."

"Come on," you say.

He chuckles slightly. "Well, your ex-husband would be right, except I've never had the pleasure of seeing you angry. Let's see. Leaves things strewn around the room . . ." He begins ticking things off his fingers. "Too many shoes. Laughs at her own jokes. Praises her own cooking. Swears at other drivers."

"When did I swear at other drivers?" you ask. "That's absolutely wrong."

"Los Angeles," he says. He continues counting. "Hates criticism, gloats when she wins at chess, always has to have sex, and eats and drinks with a little bit too much abandon." The professor puts an arm around you and squeezes. "Not bad," he says, "for an American."

"On your list of defects," you say, "you forgot to say that you are a snob. And a womanizer."

"My dear," he says, "those are my best qualities."

That evening, on the bus to the town of Essouira, you watch the sun go down on the umber plains. You ride for a while with your head on his shoulder, the bus jerking you upright now and then.

"You know," you tell him, thinking about your earlier conversation, "it's funny but I don't think I even know what my ex-husband would say were my defects. In some ways, I didn't know him that well."

"Well, that story is over."

"I wonder about that story," you say. "I'm not sure I'll ever understand it." You lean back against the professor, quiet for a few more miles. "He and his girlfriend are having a baby," you tell him.

"Who?" he asks.

"My ex-husband. And the woman he left me for. They're having a baby. Someone who knows them told me."

"Well," says the professor, stroking your arm, "that doesn't concern you."

"It's a little difficult," you say. You look out at the roadside village you are passing, and at the blank landscape beyond, tears coming to your eyes.

"I'm sorry," says the professor.

"It isn't that I still wish I'd had a baby with him," you say. "It isn't just that I'd hoped to have a baby, period, and I wasted so many precious years with him, and now I'm getting to be too old. It's that it really fucked with my story."

"What do you mean?"

"I told myself that the reason my husband left me was that he was freaked out about having a child, since he'd had a difficult childhood that he was afraid to repeat, afraid that he might, in turn, abandon his own child. And now he's having a child with her. It doesn't make sense with my story. Now it seems like the only reason he left me was that he didn't love me."

The professor touches your hair. "Maybe that story was true when you broke up," he says. "And maybe you needed to tell yourself a story that made sense when nothing else did. But you don't know what's happened between them, what has changed. You don't enter into it anymore. And your story about what happened has changed, too."

You ride along in silence for a while .

"The truth," you say, sleepily, "is that it didn't work out. He never had the sense of *la bella vita* that I have."

"Brava," says the professor, and presses his lips against your head.

You arrive in Essouira, a small town on the coast with ancient whitewashed houses, palm trees, and a few scattered minarets, and you walk into the walled medina to your hotel. You open the huge scarred door and realize you have found another hidden gem. Inside is a large courtyard with stone arches, cool green plants in terra-cotta pots, a fountain filled with roses, and a balcony with geraniums spilling over its sides. The tables and floor are covered with sea-colored Moroccan tiles, and red-hued rugs are spread here and there. Your room is tiny and charming, with a sunken canopied bed.

For the next two days, Essouria is a perfect place to *far niente*. You laze around in bed, explore the souks in the medina, walk along the beach, and eat fresh fish at outdoor grills by the ocean. You are having a lunch of sardines when the professor spots a moray eel among the day's catch. He asks for a piece of it, grilled, and gives it to you, helping you get revenge.

You nap and eat and wander and relax. You do nothing for days, but it seems like you don't even have time to write post-cards. When it's time to leave, too soon, you make your way back to Casablanca, stopping for a night at El Jadida, a small town with Portuguese ramparts and a beach. You end up in an anony-mous hotel on the beach, where you spend your last night to-gether, cuddled up, so used to each other, with a strain of sadness between you.

In the morning, you take a taxi to Casablanca. You stop off at your hotel, since your flight is the next morning. He leaves the pretty rug he had bought for himself with you, as a present. He won't let you refuse it. You drop your bags in the room and leave, since you just have time for lunch before he has to make his flight.

You return to the traditional Moroccan restaurant you went to on your first night together in Casablanca. You order almost all the same dishes, a combination of salads, eggplant, and pigeon pastilla. You sit on the same side of the banquette, an awareness running through you that this is your last lunch, trying to savor it, and anxious, in some ways, for it to be over.

You finish the meal with tea, and the professor holds your hand. "I always wonder," he says, "whether I will see you again."

"You always say that, professor," you say. "And then you say, it's not a question of *if* you see each other again, but when and where."

"I'm not so sure," he says. He squeezes your hand. "You've changed since I've known you. I think you're ready to fall in love. You weren't before, you were too heartbroken, but now, I think, you will. I'll get a letter from you saying you have a boyfriend, and maybe a baby, and that will be the end of the professor."

You sip your sweet tea.

You don't say anything. You have to admit that is a possibility. You want to believe that you could always live *la bella vita,* always be ready for a *rendez-vous* with the Parisian professor. But you also know that while you want someone with the professor's love for life, you also want someone who will be able to really share it with you, to sleep in your bed, night after night. You are ready—thanks, partly, to the professor—for a serious love, all your own.

"We could still have a little fling," you say, "in a *pied-à-terre* in Paris or something."

You look at each other, searching. And you both know that isn't true.

You leave the restaurant and hail a taxi to take him to the station to catch a train to the airport. You go along with him.

"How are you?" he asks you in the cab.

"*Ça va,*" you say, sprinkling your Italian with French, the way the professor tosses around his new English words.

"We have become experts at meeting and at parting," he says.

"It isn't easy," you say.

"No."

You arrive at the train station and find that, for all his mania for train schedules, you have just missed the one to the airport. You walk to the taxi stand, shivering a little in the fog that has descended on Casablanca since you arrived. You find a beat-up Mercedes cab, waiting to leave.

"*Ciao,*" you say, and kiss him on both cheeks. You want to tell him to remember that there is always someone far away who loves him, but the taxi driver is becoming impatient.

The professor hugs you, holding you tight for a long time. "Good-bye, Laura," he says.

You nod, you can't speak, and kiss him again on the cheek. He gets into the cab, shuts the door, and the gray Mercedes disappears down the street.

SAN FRANCISCO

It is a rare summer day in San Francisco, warm enough to ride a bicycle around without a jacket. A slight breeze sweeps the air and makes the city smell faintly of the ocean. You pedal down a leafy street in your neighborhood, past long blocks of Victorians, to your office near the city center.

Along the way, you think about the conversation you had the evening before, with Jon. His grandmother, who was dear to you, had just died, and you wanted to call someone who had loved her to say you were sorry. You'd been nervous about calling Jon at home, but you dialed their number anyway.

He was surprised to hear from you, guarded but cordial. You told him how much you would miss his grandmother. Then you congratulated him: you'd heard he'd had a baby girl. You asked the baby's name, which was more than you wanted to know, but the small talk made the conversation easier.

Now that his grandmother was gone, you finally told him, everyone you had known from your life together was gone, so now it seemed as if your whole relationship had never happened at all.

He was quiet for a long while, then said he didn't feel that way. He was still confused about what had happened between you, full of regrets and questions he couldn't answer. But that didn't take away from the fact that you had spent four years together. "We were such good friends," he ventured.

Something had broken in his reserve, and you did hear, again, the familiar voice of a friend. Conversation with him was like a drug, you thought, quoting what was once your favorite Lucinda Williams song. You talked for an hour—for the first time, without anger or recrimination. You listened to each other tell your different stories about why you had split apart.

You had both tried too hard to please each other, he concluded. He had married you because you'd wanted to be married, even though deep-down he had known he was ambivalent. He was afraid of losing you. He had genuinely been confused about whether his ambivalence was about marriage in general, or about you. But by marrying you, he said, he had done you a disservice.

Disservice, you thought. That was as close to an apology as you would ever get, so you figured you would have to accept it.

You told him you'd tried too hard to please him, too. Now you were much happier; you were much more yourself without him. Frankly, you said, he'd been too controlling. "You should see me," you told him. "I wear a lot of bright colors—never navy blue—and you would hate all of my shoes. Right now, for instance, I've got on pink and silver bowling shoes." You dangled your feet off the sofa while you talked.

He laughed. "Good for you," he said warmly.

The conversation wound down. "I think we were just never very well suited to each other," you say. "But we *were* good friends."

He wished you well, and for the first time, you wished him the same.

That next morning, you feel light and cheerful. You're glad you were able to talk to each other. Someday, you'll be able to reclaim part of those four years with him as happy memories. They weren't completely lost. And you hadn't been completely crazy to marry him in the first place. He wasn't such a bad guy, just not the right guy. He had tried. That mattered.

You roll down a steep hill, your thoughts turning to your next vacation. Maybe you could go to Mexico, you think, kayaking in Baja with friends. Or perhaps you could learn French somewhere, so you could travel more easily the next time you were in Africa. You've never traveled in Central America, either, or any part of Asia. Then again, you've never been to Sardinia, and you hardly skimmed the surface of Naples.

You brake your bicycle at a stop sign, and roll up next to another bicyclist.

"Beautiful morning," you say.

"Gorgeous," he replies, and you both pedal on.

AUTHOR'S NOTE

This is a true story. However, the names and identifying characteristics of many of the people described in this book have been changed to protect their privacy.

ACKNOWLEDGMENTS

I'm grateful to many people for helping me with this book. Among them, Don George and Salon.com first published my travel stories, and encouraged me to write more. Ethan Watters suggested I turn those stories into a book. Other members of the San Francisco Writers' Grotto, especially Mary Roach and Lisa Margonelli, provided lively commentary along the way. Jim Boylan and Ethan Canin offered generous advice on the pages they read. Thanks to my agent, Sarah Lazin, for her good sense, and to her associates, Cory Halaby and Paula Balzer. Zoe Rosenfeld was an invaluable reader. I was lucky my manuscript fell into the hands of Dawn Davis, an extraordinary editor. Grazie mille to Tonia Prencipe for her Italian perspective, and to Tom Erikson, Monica Pasqual, Cecilia Brunazzi, Cristina Taccone, and my uncle, John Gould, for their warm support. And thanks to my parents, Dr. Charles and Virginia Fraser, for always wanting me to call home, wherever I am.